Romantic

A COMEDY IN T

By Bernard Slade

SAMUEL FRENCH, INC.
45 WEST 25TH STREET   NEW YORK 10010
7623 SUNSET BOULEVARD HOLLYWOOD 90046
LONDON   TORONTO

ROMANTIC COMEDY by Bernard Slade. Opening Night, November 8, 1979. Directed by Joseph Hardy; scenery by Douglas W. Schmidt; costumes by Jane Greenwood; lighting by Tharon Musser; production stage manager, Warren Crane. Presented by Morton Gottlieb; associate producers, Ben Rosenberg and Warren Crane, in association with Thornhill Productions Inc. At the Etthel Barrymore Theater, 243 West 47th Street.

THE CAST

JASON CARMICHAEL . . . . *Anthony Perkins*

BLANCHE DAILEY . . . . *Carole Cook*

PHOEBE Craddock . . . . *Mia Farrow*

ALLISON ST. JAMES . . . . *Holly Palance*

LEO JANOWITZ . . . . *Greg Mullavey*

KATE MALLORY . . . . *Deborah May*

CAST
(in order of appearance)

Jason Carmichael

Blanche Dailey

Phoebe Craddock

Allison St. James

Leo Janowitz

Kate Mallory

SETTING

The entire action of the play takes place in the study of Jason Carmichael's New York townhouse.

ACT ONE

SCENE 1: A spring morning in the mid-sixties.
SCENE 2: Late night, a year later.

ACT TWO

SCENE 1: A November morning, ten years later.
SCENE 2: Late afternoon, six weeks later.

ACT THREE

SCENE 1: A mid-September morning, two years later.
SCENE 2: Late afternoon, three weeks later.
SCENE 3: The next morning.

Romantic Comedy

ACT ONE

SCENE 1

THE TIME: *A spring morning in 1965.*

THE SETTING: *The spacious study of* JASON CARMICHAEL's
*New York townhouse. The Back wall contains a win-
dow that looks out onto the garden, there are double
doors Stage Left that lead to the hall and a door
Stage Right leads to a non-visible dressing room. The
room is furnished with the usual number of sofas,
chairs, coffee and end tables and there is an antique
desk Upstage Center that contains some neatly-stacked
scripts, papers, and a telephone. Some of the walls
are booklined and the study projects an aura of warm,
tasteful, traditional elegance.*

AT RISE: *The PHONE is RINGING in the unoccupied
room. After a moment,* JASON CARMICHAEL *enters
from the dressing room. He is, as always, impeccably
attired, at the moment in a dressing gown, ascot,
slacks and slippers. He is carrying a well-tailored
blue suit. At this point in time, in his mid-thirties,
he is not conventionally handsome but, despite his
crumpled face, possesses a mixture of arrogance,
charm and sophistication that gives him a certain
magnetism.*

JASON. (*Irritably muttering to himself.*) I really wish
someone would get that.

7

(*Apparently someone does, as the PHONE STOPS RING-
ING.* BLANCHE DAILEY *opens the double doors and
pokes her head into the room. Flamboyant in manner
and dress, she admits to forty-two, looks fiftyish, is
actually fifty-four. Thrice married, an ex-showgirl, but
for many years a literary agent, she is nobody's fool.*)

BLANCHE. (*Surprised.*) Why aren't you dressed?

JASON. My club's sending Boris—or someone over to
give me a rubdown.

BLANCHE. (*She enters, closing doors behind her.*) Isn't
that a bit redundant on your wedding day? What are you
doing holed up in here anyway?

JASON. Allison's parents and some of her assorted relatives are staying in the upstairs rooms so I've been sleeping
in the dressing room. How's the house?

BLANCHE. Filling up. And, at the risk of introducing a
somber note into this festive affair, costing you a bundle
you can ill afford.

JASON. (*Quietly.*) God, you're crass.

BLANCHE. (*Unmoved.*) I'm supposed to be. I'm your
agent. (*Looking at suits.*) You know your problem, Jason?
You came out of your mother's womb yelling "I'll take one
in every color."

JASON. What do you want? You have an ulterior look
about you.

BLANCHE. Well, for one thing, I wanted to audition the
costume. (*She does a model's twirl.*) Very restrained for an
old Follies girl, right?

JASON. Blanche, you have a choice. You can either be a
Follies girl or you can be forty-two years old. You cannot
be both.

BLANCHE. I hate people with mathematical minds. (*The
PHONE RINGS and* BLANCHE *picks it up. Into phone.*)
Jason Carmichael's residence—Yes, he is—Oh—Hold on a
minute, please. (*She holds out the phone to him.*) Long

distance. (*He takes phone. She moves to pour herself a drink.*)

JASON. (*Into phone.*) Yes? (*His tone changes.*) Oh, hello—No, you're not the *last* person I expected to hear from but I have had more thrilling beginnings to my day— Yes, I got your messages—Because, frankly, I didn't see any point in talking to you. (*Becoming agitated.*) Look, you were the one who walked out, not me!— It wasn't what you did, it was the way you did it. If you'd been open with me instead of sneaking around behind—Oh, come on, you'd been meeting with him for over three months. Christ, we were together for *eleven* years and I had to find out by reading it in a column! (*He regains some control.*) I agree. No point at all so I'm going to hang up now. I have a very busy schedule today—I'm going to have a massage and then get married—Well, maybe someday we'll be able to sit down and laugh over it but I think you should know I don't plan on ever becoming that mellow. (*Very upset, he hangs up and turns to look at* BLANCHE.)

BLANCHE. Marty?

JASON. Can you imagine the gall of that man? After all that's happened?

BLANCHE. Jason, he was your writing partner, not your wife. You sound like a jilted lover.

JASON. Why shouldn't I feel jilted? The man was meeting with some film producer behind my back working on a *screenplay!*

BLANCHE. I'm sure he wanted you to work on it with him but he knew you'd never move to L.A.

JASON. I'm too young to start writing about real life from memory.

BLANCHE. Since when did you write about real life?

JASON. (*Very agitated.*) My God do you know what I went through with that man for eleven years? He always exuded a strange musty smell that positively made your head reel. Did you ever notice that?

BLANCHE. You'll find someone else.

JASON. (*A sudden change of mood; sadly.*) No, I'll never find another partner like Marty. Why did he do it, Blanche?

BLANCHE. (*Shrugs.*) Oh, I don't know—I always got the feeling Marty felt overshadowed by you. Maybe he just wanted his own identity.

JASON. Who could confuse us? The man was five feet tall and had a small clump of hair growing out of the bridge of his nose.

BLANCHE. (*She watches him as he moves to pour himself a healthy drink.*) I sense a certain panic in you, Jason. What is it?

JASON. (*He turns to look at her.*) Marty and I spent all our writing lives together. Together we had five smash hits, two nervous hits and one flop. Lately, I've had this persistent, nasty little thought. (*He looks at her; simply.*) Was he the talented one? (*BLANCHE is too astounded by his uncharacteristic vulnerability to reply.*) Blanche, this is no time for a pause.

BLANCHE. I always get tongue-tied when I discover someone's human.

JASON. If you let it get outside this room I'll tell everyone that's the real color of your hair. (*They embrace. He moves away.*) Where the hell is Boris? I have a knot in my shoulder that feels as if it was tied by a stevedore.

BLANCHE. You found anyone else you think you can work with?

JASON. Blanche, it's not like hiring a maid! A collaboration is a very sensitive relationship. It has all the disadvantages of a marriage and none of the advantages.

BLANCHE. What did you think of this play I sent you— "The Girl In The Back Seat"?

JASON. Oh, I don't know—I only half read it—I suppose it has a certain quaint charm but I'm in no mood to make any decisions right now.

BLANCHE. Well, I think it has great possibilities and the author wanted you to read it. His name is P. J. Craddock.

JASON. What kind of name is that?

BLANCHE. Probably a real one. We've just corresponded so I don't know a damn thing about him except that he teaches school somewhere up in Vermont. Look, why don't you take the script along on your honeymoon? It'll help fill in the awkward pauses. The author's coming into town a week from today and I've set up a meeting with him here at eleven o'clock. Okay?

JASON. What makes you think we'll have awkward pauses?

BLANCHE. What? Oh, just a figure of speech.

JASON. I thought you liked Allison.

BLANCHE. I adore Allison.

JASON. Did I tell you her father was the Ambassador to New Zealand?

BLANCHE. Not in the last ten minutes. Why are you so impressed?

JASON. Blanche, the man has a *flag* on his car.

BLANCHE. Is that why you're getting married, Jason? So you can double-park in downtown Auckland?

JASON. (*After a slight pause.*) Allison has some rare qualities, you know. She's unspoiled, sweet, giving, spontaneous. All the things I'm not.

BLANCHE. Honest, but hardly a reason for marriage.

JASON. All right. I'll be thirty-five next month. I want a family before I get too old. (*A slight shrug.*) The timing's right.

BLANCHE. It's still not too late to call the whole thing off and send everyone home, you know.

JASON. Just like in "Philadelphia Story"? People don't do that in real life.

BLANCHE. (*Stands.*) Well—if there's not going to be any drama I may as well get drunk. (*She moves to the door.*)

JASON. Tell the maid to keep everyone out of here, will you? The only person I want to see is a masseur.

BLANCHE. Jason, are you *sure* you want to go through with this?

JASON. Of course I'm not. Is anybody just before their wedding? (*A beat.*) But I'm sure of one thing. This marriage is going to work.

BLANCHE. How do you know?

JASON. I'm a perfectionist.

BLANCHE. (*She looks at him for a moment. Gently.*) Break a leg, kid.

(*She exits.* JASON *stands for a moment before he exits to the dressing room leaving the suit on the sofa. After a moment, the double doors open and* PHOEBE *enters. She is holding an overstuffed, scuffed tote purse. We will later see that she is quite pretty but if* JASON *has made the best of his looks, she has made the worst. At this point in her mid-twenties she is inclined to cover her basic shyness with a somewhat self-conscious forthright manner. Right now she is totally overawed by her surroundings and stands drinking in the room. After a few moments she summons up enough courage to move back to the desk, tentatively touches the manuscripts. Finally, she slowly sits, not quite believing she is sitting at* JASON CARMICHAEL'S *desk. The PHONE RINGS. She stands and stares at it.*)

JASON. (*Offstage.*) I'd really appreciate it if someone would get that.

PHOEBE. (*She gulps and picks up phone. Into phone.*) Hello—Yes, it is—Boris called in with the flu and can't come—Yes, I'll—I'll pass on that message.

(*She hangs up. At this point* JASON *enters from the dressing room. He is totally nude.* Oblivious to* PHOEBE, *who is in a frozen state of shock,* JASON *carries a portable*

---

* It is not absolutely essential that the actor playing Jason be nude in this scene, only that he appear to be nude. This effect can be achieved by staging the scene so that the massage table or the chair partially shields the actor from the audience.

*massage table which partially shields his body from
the audience. He turns Upstage, and moves towards
the desk but stops in his tracks as he sees* PHOEBE. *His
back is now three-quarters to the audience, she is in
front of the desk, facing the audience; staring fixedly at*
JASON's *hairline, trying to appear unruffled. There is a
pause.*)

JASON. (*Calmly.*) Where's Boris?
PHOEBE. Oh, Boris couldn't come.
JASON. Oh. (*A pause.*)
PHOEBE. I'm—overawed. (*Another pause.*)
JASON. (*Finally.*) Thank you.
PHOEBE. You're younger looking than your photos. (*Too
brightly.*) Of course most of those were head shots. Ha, ha.
What a dumb thing to say! I have this cousin who writes me
letters and always puts ha ha after anything she means to be
funny. May I ask a question?
JASON. Of course.
PHOEBE. Are you naked?
JASON. Either that or I'm standing in a very severe draft.
PHOEBE. You're just a white blob to me. I'm not wearing
my glasses. I have very weak eyes.
JASON. Well, I hope you have strong hands.
PHOEBE. Strong hands?
JASON. I have a knot in my shoulder. Do you think you
can do anything about it?
PHOEBE. Well—I don't know. I can try— (*She speaks in
an even stream of words.*) but first I'd like to say that I've
seen all your plays and admired your work for many years.
In fact, at the risk of sounding gushy, I might say I've
idolized your talent. Over the years you and your partner
have brightened one's days, molded one's tastes, and although impossible to attain, provided one with a standard of
civilized behavior. (*There is a longish pause.*)
JASON. (*Finally.*) You're not the masseur.
PHOEBE. You thought I was?

JASON. I rarely receive guests in the buff.

PHOEBE. I'm very relieved to hear that. I mean I'm trying to appear unruffled and chic but underneath I'm a terrible prude.

JASON. Look, I don't want to appear churlish but I'm getting rather chilly. Who are you?

PHOEBE. Oh, I'm The Girl In The Back Seat. (*A beat.*) P. J. Craddock. But my given name is Phoebe.

JASON. You're a week early.

PHOEBE. No, it's today. (*Happy to get out of his line of vision she moves around to extract a letter from her purse. He does not move.*) I have the letter right here. It's a bit grubby from constant reading but—here. (*She hands it to him. He glances at it.*)

JASON. Uh—would you excuse me for a moment?

PHOEBE. (*In a flurry of activity, she quickly gathers up her purse.*) Gladly! (*She makes for the door, stops, awkwardly tries to lighten the situation.*) It's funny, one's fantasies never turn out quite how one expects, do they? I mean, I'd always visualized you wearing a sports coat. (*She makes a rather awkward exit.*)

(JASON *puts the letter on the sofa, very calmly puts on his shorts, and shirt, and crosses to the mirror. He is looking into the mirror when his calm exterior shatters.*)

JASON. That—was—the—most—*embarrassing experience of my life!!!* (*He lets out an anguished yell and, overcome by the embarrassment of it all proceeds to go into a jerky, strange, maniacal, hopping series of movements or dance around the room, all the time muttering.*) God—that was embarrassing! Totally—embarrassing! Standing there naked like an idiot—*embarrassing!* Completely and utterly— (*He stops as he sees that* PHOEBE, *clutching her purse has opened the door and is staring at him; an odd expression on her face.*)

PHOEBE. I'm sorry. I thought I heard you yelling as if you were in pain.

JASON. (*Extremely calm and polite again.*) No, I'm all right, thank you.

PHOEBE. Oh. Well, excuse me again. (*She exits.*)

JASON. (*Looks heavenward for a moment before letting out a low, heartfelt expletive.*) Oh—shit!! (*He pulls himself together, puts on trousers, and crosses to doors and opens them to admit* PHOEBE.)

PHOEBE. Look, perhaps I should come back at the Easter break.

JASON. (*Drily.*) Why? We're having so much fun.

PHOEBE. Well, they seem to be preparing for some sort of function out there.

JASON. I'm sorry, Miss Craddock, I'm afraid you've caught me at an awkward time.

PHOEBE. Yes, there's a hippopotamus in the room isn't there? It's an expression. There's something present that neither of us wants to acknowledge. But we both know it's there, don't we?

JASON. We do?

PHOEBE. I've been thinking about what you were doing when I came back in here just now.

JASON. Miss Craddock, I really don't think it's necessary to—

PHOEBE. No, I believe we should bring it out in the open. You were dancing around the room in a bizarre fashion and uttering odd, guttural sounds. Well, I want you to know that I don't think any the worse of you for that.

JASON. Thank you.

PHOEBE. Sometimes when I'm alone in the classroom I hook my feet over a rafter, hang upside down and sing "Night And Day." I mean we all do peculiar things when we're alone.

JASON. (*Despite himself, he is touched by her kindness and starts to become intrigued by her.*) You're very kind.

PHOEBE. (*She becomes uncomfortable under his gaze.*) I feel like an idiot. There's perspiration trickling down my back and the strap on my slip has broken.

JASON. There's no need for you to have told me that.

PHOEBE. Bad habit.

JASON. What?

PHOEBE. Telling people before they notice it themselves. You know, "I'm Phoebe Craddock, I have squinty eyes and I'm messy looking but I hope you like me anyway."

JASON. You said you've seen all my plays?

PHOEBE. Twenty-eight times.

JASON. Each?

PHOEBE. In Boston—when you were trying out. I put myself through school working as an usher at the Colonial Theater.

JASON. Ushers usually don't watch plays. They sit in the lobby and talk too loudly.

PHOEBE. Not me. I saw everything but I always liked the romantic comedies best. I mean I realize they weren't representative of the real world as we know it—at least as I know it—there isn't an abundance of elegance or wit where I was raised—I mean you could go a lifetime in my neighborhood without anyone saying anything you'd want to put in a play. Shut up, Phoebe.

JASON. I beg your pardon?

PHOEBE. I suppose I feel if I keep talking I won't have to hear what you have to say about my play.

JASON. I'm sorry. I haven't had time to really read it yet. (*There is a slight pause.*)

PHOEBE. May I sit for a moment?

JASON. Of course.

PHOEBE. Thank you. I feel a little faint. From *relief.* Isn't that silly?

JASON. (*Gently.*) No, I understand perfectly. It's no fun being naked.

PHOEBE. It's quite curious. Did you know one's knees

actually do knock when one is apprehensive? (*He is staring at her.*) Is there lipstick on my teeth?

JASON. What? Oh, no. I have this strange feeling we've met before.

PHOEBE. We have. It was about five years ago. You were trying out "Blue Is For Boys." Between the Wednesday matinee and evening performance I was in the Union Oyster House. You came in and sat at the only empty table, which happened to be right next to mine. Well, naturally I was thrilled and in a burst of girlish impetuousness I turned and blurted out a stream of totally incoherent compliments about how much I admired your work. You were very nice, listened politely and said "thank you." Still trembling from the encounter I turned away. I was drinking hot chocolate— you know with those small marshmallows floating on top? I had just taken a gulp when you suddenly said, "And what do you do?" The hot chocolate went down the wrong way, I choked slightly, and as I looked at you, I realized I had small marshmallows shooting out of my nose. You looked at me for a moment and then, very gravely, you said, "You know, not many people can do that."

JASON. It seems that our meetings are not destined to go smoothly.

PHOEBE. Not at all the way the characters in your plays would meet.

JASON. Only because I didn't think of it. (*They smile at one another.*)

PHOEBE. Do you need any help?

JASON. In my career?

PHOEBE. With your cuff links.

JASON. Thank you.

(*She crosses to him, bends over to thread the cuff links. JASON, conscious of her closeness, is staring at her. She looks up.*)

PHOEBE. I'm sorry, I'm all thumbs. (*She notices his stare.*) What is it?

JASON. You don't smell musty.

PHOEBE. (*At a loss.*) Uh—thank you.

JASON. My ex-partner smelled musty.

PHOEBE. (*Puzzled.*) He wasn't that old was he?

JASON. No.

PHOEBE. (*She goes back to putting the cuff links in.*) I'm afraid I've crumpled your cuff.

(JASON *is looking at her with an odd, incredulous expression. Disturbed and somewhat bewildered by his reaction to her, he abruptly picks up her script, flips it open.*)

JASON. Why did you want me to read your play?

PHOEBE. I stole the leading character from you.

JASON. (*He looks up from the script.*) Which one?

PHOEBE. The girl you used to write in the fifties. The high-spirited but basically "nice" girl who always faced the dilemma of whether to forfeit her virginity or hold onto it until the final curtain. You remember her?

JASON. Of course. Patti—Sally—Mary.

PHOEBE. (*A thought hits her.*) Why did they all have such short names?

JASON. They're easy to type. (*He goes back to reading script.*)

PHOEBE. Ah. Well, whatever happened to her?

JASON. She always successfully defended her virginity, married the leading man, moved to Scarsdale, had 2.7 children and lived happily ever after.

PHOEBE. (*Nervously—very aware of him reading her script.*) Exactly. But what if she didn't live happily ever after? Supposing twenty years later—today—she went through a divorce. Now in her late thirties, still attractive, she's suddenly single again and is plunged into an entirely new world with a whole new sexual morality. How does she cope with that?

JASON. ''The Girl In The Back Seat.''

PHOEBE. Well, that's where most of us ended up fighting for our honor, isn't it?

JASON. (*He looks at her.*) What do you know about fifties' sexual mores? Aren't you part of the permissive sixties?

PHOEBE. No, I'm extremely backward. I mean in that way. Anyway, I borrowed your character, added twenty years and took it from there.

JASON. You don't know how to construct a scene and your dialogue is stilted.

PHOEBE. You can tell all that from three pages?

JASON. (*Testily.*) Look, I do hope you're not going to be—*sensitive!*

PHOEBE. Why do you say my dialogue is stilted?

JASON. The girl says ''purchase'' instead of ''buy,'' ''obtain'' instead of ''get'' and ''plight'' instead of ''trouble.'' People don't talk like that.

PHOEBE. I do.

JASON. You're an English teacher from a small village in Vermont and I have the suspicion you're quite eccentric.

PHOEBE. Spotted that did you?

JASON. You know that about yourself?

PHOEBE. No. I only said it because I didn't want to appear sensitive.

JASON. (*Impatiently.*) Look, when I said you were eccentric I meant it as a compliment!

PHOEBE. Thank you. I think you're eccentric too.

JASON. Why?

PHOEBE. You do peculiar things when you're alone.

JASON. So do you.

PHOEBE. No, I don't. I made that up to lessen your embarrassment.

JASON. Miss Craddock, you have a warped view of life.

PHOEBE. Another compliment?

JASON. Essential for someone who wants to write comedy. But it's only a start.

PHOEBE. (*She moves to collect her things.*) Yes, well, I certainly appreciate your taking the time to see me. (*She starts for the door.*)

JASON. Would you stop teaching and move to New York to work with me?

PHOEBE. (*She turns.*) I thought you hated my play?

JASON. Why would you think that?

PHOEBE. You said I didn't know how to construct a scene and my dialogue was stilted.

JASON. *My* dialogue is brilliant.

PHOEBE. You really want to work with me?

JASON. I'm not sure yet. Look, you'd better sit down. (*She does. His manner is still brusque.*) Miss Craddock, what do you think the theatre is?

PHOEBE. A celebration of the human condition.

JASON. (*Impatiently.*) No, that's not what I'm talking about. Are you single?

PHOEBE. Yes.

JASON. Do you plan on getting married?

PHOEBE. Eventually.

JASON. That's not good enough.

PHOEBE. I didn't know this was an exam.

JASON. Look, I don't plan on us becoming Will and Ariel Durant. But I don't want to invest in a partnership and then have you suddenly get the urge to become a nursing mother.

PHOEBE. I see.

JASON. No, you don't. You don't know a damn thing about the theatre. The working conditions are intolerable, the people you have to deal with are egocentric maniacs, and it's filled with rejections on every level. When you're writing comedy the opposite of success is not failure—it's embarrassment. And it's very public. They write headlines, Miss Craddock! (*He is unhappy with his knot, tears it apart and starts again.*) All right, that's the pleasant part. You'll be working with me and I am a difficult person. In fact, some people think I am *impossible*. I am demanding, selfish, obsessive, moody, arrogant, rarely satisfied and my own mother once said I lack warmth. Would you be willing to accept those conditions?

PHOEBE. Sounds like a lot of fun.

JASON. All right, dammit, we'll give it a try! (*He angrily turns away again.*)

PHOEBE. I just have one question. (*He looks at her.*) Why are you so *angry?* (*There is a pause.*)

JASON. (*Finally—quietly.*) Well, what do you expect? You barge in here unannounced, disrupt my life, and then have the gall to be talented. (*She doesn't know what to say to this.*) I'm sorry. It's—your timing. I'd made certain— plans. (*She is still puzzled. Evasively.*) Also this damned tie won't tie.

PHOEBE. Maybe I can help. (*She moves to him, knots tie through following.*) My mother died when I was young so I've been tying my father's and three brothers' ties for years. I can cook, darn socks, even cut hair if required.

JASON. (*Conscious of her closeness.*) A simple Windsor knot will do for now.

PHOEBE. (*She finishes knotting the tie, pats it in place.*) There. (*They are standing very close, both now aware of the current between them.*)

JASON. (*With a tone of quiet disbelief.*) You're not my type at all you know.

(*The moment is shattered as* ALLISON ST. JAMES, *in a bridal dress and veil, enters the room. She is a beautiful, friendly, young woman with an open, direct manner. She stops and surveys the two.*)

ALLISON. Fine state of affairs. Two minutes before our wedding I discover my fiancé with another woman.

JASON. (*Flustered.*) Allison, you shouldn't be here.

ALLISON. Oh, I don't believe in those old superstitions. (*She moves to him, kisses him.*) I just had to find out if you're as terrified as I am. (*She slips her arm through his, smiles at the stunned* PHOEBE.) I don't believe we've met.

JASON. (*Very flustered.*) I'm sorry. Miss— (*Goes blank on her name.*) uh—I'd like you to meet—uh— (*He goes blank again.*) My fiancée.

ALLISON. (*Amused at his nervousness.*) Allison. I didn't catch *your* name.

PHOEBE. Craddock—P. J.—Phoebe.

JASON. Miss Craddock—is going to be my new writing partner.

ALLISON. When did this happen?

JASON. What happen? Oh, just today.

ALLISON. That's marvelous! We'll have the same anniversary. (*They stare at her.*) Your partnership and our marriage. We'll be able to all celebrate together. (*To* PHOEBE.) You're staying for the wedding I hope.

JASON. Her?

ALLISON. Darling, I know *you* are. (*To* PHOEBE.) I'll throw you the bouquet.

PHOEBE. I'm sorry—I'm from Vermont. (ALLISON *is puzzled.*)

JASON. It was Blanche's fault. She came a week early. And she's a woman.

ALLISON. (*Not understanding.*) That's—too bad. (*To* JASON—*playfully.*) Well, sir—what do you think? Still want to go through with this thing?

JASON. Yes—well, I've had trouble tying my tie. (*He moves away to put on his jacket.*)

ALLISON. Jason, did you know you're not making any sense at all?

JASON. I'm not?

ALLISON. That's okay. You've made me feel better.

JASON. Oh?

ALLISON. You're obviously as terrified as I am. (*She moves to door, turns.*) I hope we'll be good friends, Phoebe. (*To* JASON.) As for you—I'll see you around, huh? (*She blows him a kiss and exits.*)

PHOEBE. (*Finally.*) She's very beautiful.

JASON. Yes.

PHOEBE. She seems nice.

JASON. She is, actually.

PHOEBE. Lively.

JASON. Very.

PHOEBE. She's obviously very fond of you. Well— naturally.

JASON. Hmm.

PHOEBE. Very flat, Norfolk.

JASON. (*He looks at her.*) What?

PHOEBE. We were sounding very Noel Cowardish. It's a line from one of his plays.

JASON. "Private Lives."

PHOEBE. First scene.

JASON. They met on their respective honeymoons, fell in love, and ran away together at the end of the first act. (*A beat.*) Marvelous.

PHOEBE. And he made it totally believable.

JASON. Anything's believable if it's done well. (*They look at one another for a moment.*) Would you like a drink?

PHOEBE. (*Gratefully.*) Yes, I really would.

JASON. (*He moves to pour two drinks.*) Scotch?

PHOEBE. It doesn't matter. I don't drink. (*He turns to look at her.*) It seems—fitting. (*Finally.*) It's been quite a day.

JASON. Oh?

PHOEBE. Well, I meet my girlhood idol, he asks me to work with him; and then rushes off to get married. (*A beat.*) Extraordinary.

JASON. Oh, I don't know. Boy meets girl, boy gets girl, boy loses girl. Been done a million times. (*They are gazing at one another as* BLANCHE *enters through the double doors.*)

BLANCHE. Places please. Let's get this show on the road. (*She stops as she sees* PHOEBE.) Who's she?

JASON. Long story. I'll explain later.

BLANCHE. Well, it's now or never, kid.

JASON. I'll be right there. (BLANCHE *exits.* JASON *holds his glass up in a toast. Finally.*) Phoebe—to us.

(*They both drink. He puts his glass down, moves to the double doors, opens them. We hear a LOW MURMUR from outside. He looks out the door. Slowly he turns and looks at* PHOEBE. *They are in this position as the—CURTAIN FALLS.*)

END OF SCENE 1, ACT ONE

ACT ONE

SCENE 2

THE TIME: *A year later. Very late at night.*

AT RISE: *It is raining outside. The Stage is dark except for a small pool of light which emanates from an end table lamp and illuminates* JASON *who is sitting on the sofa, a folded* New York Times *beside him. He is wearing an overcoat and scarf and is steadily drinking from a large tumbler of Scotch, his face impassive. He shows no sign of drunkenness.* BLANCHE, *dressed in a fur coat over evening wear, appears in the doorway, regards him for a moment.*

BLANCHE. Is getting drunk the answer?

JASON. No, but it makes you forget the question.

BLANCHE. (*She touches a light switch and some other lamps go on.*) The *audience* really loved it, Jason.

JASON. (*A statement.*) You saw the *Times* notice.

BLANCHE. (*She gives a little shrug, removes her fur coat, moves to deposit it.*) Listen, it'll do very well in stock. Why'd you leave the party so early?

JASON. My cheeks started to ache from smiling as if I didn't care. Felt like "Miss Rhode Island." How's Phoebe taking it?

BLANCHE. I don't know. She left right after that horrible thing she did.

JASON. What horrible thing?

BLANCHE. (*Shudders slightly.*) It's too horrible to talk about. Be nice to her, Jason. She's probably feeling very fragile.

JASON. I don't exactly feel like a Mack truck myself.

(PHOEBE *enters. She is soaking wet and is wearing a rain-coat, buttoned incorrectly, over an evening dress that has seen better days. She pauses inside the door, attempts a bright smile.*)

PHOEBE. Well, the theatre certainly is character building, isn't it?

JASON. (*He has been looking at her appearance.*) Jesus, who dresses you—Quasimodo? You okay?

PHOEBE. Well, I do have some questions.

JASON. The only answer for that is a drink.

PHOEBE. No, thank you. I believe I'm still quite "squiffed." Tonight I found out that I cannot drink.

JASON. Oh?

PHOEBE. (*Nods thoughtfully.*) I threw up on the mayor's shoes. Well, *in* the mayor's shoes. Shoe. (*She gives up on the wet buttons.*) His right shoe.

JASON. How did you manage that?

PHOEBE. He was sitting next to me at the party. He'd

taken off his right shoe. I'd had two banana daiquiris. I must say he was very nice about it.

JASON. Well, he's always been a big supporter of the Arts. (*To* BLANCHE.) Was that the horrible thing she did?

BLANCHE. No, that was later.

PHOEBE. Would you mind if I didn't talk about that for a few years?

(JASON *moves to help her out of her raincoat. He hands her purse and rain hat to* BLANCHE.)

JASON. Pull your arm out of this—no, the other arm— look, just stand still and don't do anything—that's it. (*He gets the coat off, hands it to* BLANCHE *who takes it to the library steps.*) Go and sit over there. (*He indicates the sofa.* PHOEBE *crosses to sit while* JASON *gets a lap robe from the ottoman in front of the wing chair. He crosses with it to* PHOEBE. *Nervously*—) You're not going to throw up again, are you? (*He puts the blanket around* PHOEBE'S *shoulders. He kneels to take off her wet shoes.*)

PHOEBE. No, I was just wondering why I feel like a criminal. I mean we didn't commit an actual crime, did we?

JASON. Just a misdemeanor.

PHOEBE. Then why do I feel like Lizzie Borden? Is that normal?

JASON. Oh, I think it's fairly natural. After all, the murder weapon's in full view at the Booth Theatre. Blanche, I think this girl could use some coffee. Would you tell the cook to make some? (BLANCHE *has been watching him curiously.*) What's the matter?

BLANCHE. She's very good for you, Jason. Brings out your better nature. (*She exits.*)

JASON. Don't take it too hard, kid—it's only a play. In fifty years' time only you and I will remember. And I'm not too sure about ''I.'' (*He crosses to the bar to make a drink.*)

PHOEBE. It's not only the play. It's what I did at the party in front of all those people.

JASON. Well, since it seems to be in the public domain, maybe you should tell me about it.

PHOEBE. (*In dull voice.*) There was a great deal of noise and confusion. Then someone rushed in the door with a newspaper in his hand. He shoved it at me and said "It's marvelous—it's all about you!" I scrambled up on top of a table and yelled, "Quiet everyone—I have a wonderful review from the *Times!*" (*A beat.*) Now you may be wondering why I did that.

JASON. It does seem somewhat uncharacteristic.

PHOEBE. My only excuse is that I was—overstimulated. Of course everyone immediately became silent and I began to read the review in my best, loud, clear, schoolteacher voice. Well, it was an absolutely horrendous notice. All the people were staring up at me as if I was— (*She searches for the right word.*) demented. It was—horrible. I tried skipping paragraphs—editing out the bad parts, but it was difficult because—I'm somewhat astigmatic—and there were no *good* parts. Gradually this confused—babble—filled the room and—I'm having trouble concentrating—I'd like to stop talking now.

JASON. Who was the son of a bitch who gave you the paper?

PHOEBE. My father. Oh, it wasn't his fault. He thought it was exciting just to be *mentioned*. (*She looks at him.*) Was it as humiliating as I think it was?

JASON. You feeling better now?

PHOEBE. Sleepy. Incredibly sleepy. Do you think that's the alcohol?

JASON. Either that or the bananas. (*He sits beside her on the sofa.*) Why don't you put your head down? (*Much to his surprise, she doesn't lean the other way but gratefully puts her head on his lap and closes her eyes.*) You'll be okay, kid. Oh, for a few days you'll be a little gun shy. You'll be afraid to open menus in restaurants in case there's a bad review there—but eventually the pain will go away and be replaced by something much easier to live with—bitterness.

PHOEBE. (*Sleepily.*) You're trying to make me laugh.

JASON. Not too successfully, it seems.

PHOEBE. But I appreciate—the thought. (*She seems to have drifted off to sleep. He gently strokes her hair.*)

JASON. Sweet dreams, kid.

(*At this point* ALLISON *enters. Still beautiful, tastefully dressed, she seems somewhat more cheerful than the occasion demands and we sense an underlying tension between her and* JASON. *She stops as she sees* JASON *and* PHOEBE.)

ALLISON. (*Finally.*) Do you ever get the feeling we're drifting apart?

JASON. (*Turns to look at her but continues to absently stroke* PHOEBE's *hair.*) Just comforting a comrade wounded in the field of battle.

ALLISON. That's weird. I mean usually she's so shy around you.

JASON. I think it's the liquor talking.

ALLISON. (*Sits down on the other end of the sofa, takes* PHOEBE's *feet in her lap.*) Her feet are freezing, poor dear. (*She warms her feet with her hands during the following.*) I'm sorry about the play.

JASON. You mean the notices?

ALLISON. Are they that important?

JASON. Only if you want people to buy tickets.

ALLISON. Don't patronize me, Jason. I may not know anything about the theatre but I'm not an idiot.

JASON. It's all right, Allison. I know you never liked the play.

ALLISON. It's not that I didn't like it. It's just that I didn't think it was *about* anything.

JASON. (*Wearily.*) It was about giving an audience an entertaining evening.

ALLISON. (*Looks down at* PHOEBE.) Was it that hard on her?

JASON. Allison, we just saw a year's work go down the drain. She's given up a career, spent all her savings and tonight it all blew up in her face. (*A beat.*) And how was *your* day?

ALLISON. What are you going to do?

JASON. Have an affair or buy a new hat. I'll think of something.

ALLISON. (*She regards him for a moment.*) Jason, we need to talk.

JASON. I thought we were.

ALLISON. I mean about us.

JASON. (*Finally.*) Does it have to be tonight?

ALLISON. Yes. I have something important to tell you. I've been waiting until after you got the play open. (*She gets up, moves away.*) It didn't seem fair to burden you with it before.

JASON. Suddenly I'm cold sober.

ALLISON. Well, I think we should be alone for this sort of discussion.

JASON. Then why did you bring it up now?

ALLISON. (*A trifle tartly.*) I just wanted you to pencil it in on your appointment pad. (*They are looking at one another as* BLANCHE, *carrying a tray containing coffee, enters.*)

BLANCHE. Sorry I was so long. I was on the phone to Harry, trying to get some word on the other reviews.

JASON. And?

BLANCHE. I guess they weren't in the mood for charm, Jason. (*There is a gloomy pause.*)

ALLISON. (*Finally.*) So—is it okay if I get out of my "lucky" dress now? (BLANCHE *and* JASON *both turn to look at her.*) Sorry. I was just trying to lighten the situation.

BLANCHE. You want some coffee?

ALLISON. No thanks, Blanche. I really do need to get out of these clothes. (*She moves to door, turns.*) I think Phoebe might feel better if she stayed with us tonight. I'll bring her some blankets and she can bunk down in your dressing room. (ALLISON *exits.* BLANCHE *pours coffee through following.*)

BLANCHE. She's sweet.

JASON. She's a snob.

BLANCHE. (*Surprised.*) Allison's the least snobbish person I know.

JASON. I mean about the theatre.

BLANCHE. Well, you're a snob about everything *but* the theatre. (*At this point* PHOEBE *sits bolt upright.*)

PHOEBE. Oh, my God! (*She stands up, looking very disoriented.* JASON *and* BLANCHE *have also jumped up.*)

BLANCHE. What is it?

PHOEBE. I—I had this terrible dream. I was at this opening night party and someone shoved a newspaper in my hand and— (*As the realization hits her.*) Oh, my God.

JASON. I think she's still "squiffed."

BLANCHE. (*Hands* PHOEBE *a cup of coffee.*) Here, drink this.

JASON. I'd better change. My lap feels a little warm and damp.

PHOEBE. (*Embarrassed.*) I'm terribly sorry.

JASON. That's all right. It felt quite agreeable. (*He exits to the dressing room.*)

PHOEBE. Did I pass out?

BLANCHE. No, you just went to sleep in Jason's lap.

PHOEBE. (*Stunned.*) I actually went to sleep in his *lap?* (BLANCHE *nods.*) What did he do?

BLANCHE. He stroked your hair.

PHOEBE. He stroked my *hair?* (BLANCHE *nods.*) How— odd. I mean, Jason is not a physical person. We rarely touch.

BLANCHE. Well, you touched tonight.

PHOEBE. And I missed it. (*She sips coffee for a moment.*) Do you know I never call him anything?

BLANCHE. (*Puzzled.*) What?

PHOEBE. Well, it seemed silly to call him Mr. Carmichael and although he asked me to call him Jason, I could never quite bring myself to do that.

BLANCHE. That must have made things a bit difficult when you were working together.

PHOEBE. Yes. I always had to wait until he looked at me before I could talk. Will they close the play tomorrow?

BLANCHE. Nothing lasts forever, kid. What are you going to do?

PHOEBE. Go back to the classroom, I suppose. (*A small shrug.*) It's probably all for the best.

BLANCHE. I know what you mean.

PHOEBE. (*Flustered.*) Is the way I feel about him that obvious?

BLANCHE. (*Gently.*) Only to the trained eye. Get a good night's sleep, honey. We'll talk tomorrow. (BLANCHE *crosses to get her coat.*) Oh, Jason . . . Jason, I'm leaving. I'll see you in the morning at the funeral arrangements.

(*She exits.* JASON, *wearing a dressing gown over his dinner shirt and trousers, enters. He crosses to close the door behind* BLANCHE.)

JASON. Look, would it be all right with you if I dropped the arrogant facade, got sloppy drunk and whined and sniveled a lot?

PHOEBE. I'd consider that a privilege. (*They look at one another for a moment.*)

JASON. Do me a favor, Phoebe—don't.

PHOEBE. Don't what?

JASON. Don't make a speech.

PHOEBE. How did you know I was going to make a speech?

JASON. (*He moves to pour himself a drink.*) Your eyes start to water and you get an odd, pinched look around the bridge of your nose. (*He turns to face her.*) Anyway, it's my turn.

PHOEBE. (*Surprised.*) Your turn?

JASON. Yes. (*He paces for a moment, turns to face her.*) Phoebe—don't let them get to you.

PHOEBE. (*She waits but there is no more. Incredulous.*) That's it? "Don't let them get to me?"

JASON. That's about it. I know this whole experience must have been difficult for you but—

PHOEBE. (*Emotionally.*) Difficult? The first week of rehearsal I was bitten by a rat! The second week I was mugged in the elevator—and then in Philadelphia I became quite unhinged and almost tackled a middle-aged woman around the knees to prevent her from leaving the theater. After forcing her into a seat and hissing, "You'll miss the best part!" I discovered she was one of the ushers. This whole experience was capped tonight when I regurgitated into the shoe of a public official, stood up on a table to happily announce my inadequacies to a crowd of total strangers, fell asleep in your lap and dribbled on your over-coat, and— (*Her eyes welling up.*) it was the best time I've had in my entire life!!

JASON. Then why are you crying?

PHOEBE. (*Tearfully.*) Because it's all over! (*Very touched,* JASON *sits next to her and puts his arm around her so that her head rests on his shoulder. Finally:*) I'm wetting you again.

JASON. (*Brusquely; moving away.*) Yes, and it's some-thing that should be nipped firmly in the bud. Now, if you promise to stop, I'll promise to be better next time.

PHOEBE. (*Stunned.*) Next time?

JASON. On the next play.

PHOEBE. You mean you want to go on working with me?

JASON. You think I'm going to take the rap alone?

PHOEBE. But—but I don't understand. Everyone said this play didn't have the quality of your others because of me.

JASON. They were right. (*She stares at him.*) You let me take your play, remove all the charm and sentiment and substitute jokes. If we're going to keep working together, you've got to stop letting me bully you. You're my partner, not my student, so at least once a month I suggest you tell me I'm a horse's ass. Look, if you're even *thinking* of making a speech, I'll withdraw the offer.

PHOEBE. It's not a speech. I just don't want you to do this out of loyalty—or misplaced—compassion. I realize my behavior tonight has been rather—erratic, but, actually, I'm quite resilient. I'll survive.

JASON. Well, I'm not sure I will. (*As she looks at him: Awkwardly.*) The reason I'm asking you to stay is not *only* professional. I've—I've grown—attached to you. (*Her gaze disconcerts him, causing him to blurt:*) Phoebe, Allison and I are separating.

PHOEBE. (*Absolutely stunned.*) When did this happen?

JASON. It's still only a rumor, but, as you know, bad rumors generally turn out to be true. (*Embarrassed.*) Look, I feel uncomfortable talking about this. The point is I'm going to need a friend.

PHOEBE. (*Sympathetically.*) Is there anything I can do?

JASON. (*Gently.*) Yes—go wash your face. When you come back we'll both get really drunk and convince each other that none of this is our fault.

PHOEBE. (*Moves to the dressing room door, turns, has difficulty saying his name but finally manages it.*) Jason?

JASON. Oh, God, you're really going to do it, aren't you?

PHOEBE. (*Rather formally.*) Jason, I know how any display of emotion embarrasses you, but that's all the more reason why this must be said. I—I needed someone tonight and I want to thank you for letting me be your friend.

(*She quickly exits to the dressing room.* ALLISON, *wearing a dressing gown, and carrying some blankets, enters.*)

ALLISON. Well, has my pal sobered up yet?

JASON. I wasn't drunk—just shell shocked.

ALLISON. I meant Phoebe. (*She puts blanket down, she starts to leave but at the door turns and stops.*) I've thought of a hundred ways to tell you this but—well, I suppose the best way is to keep it simple.

JASON. (*Warily.*) Always.

ALLISON. The trouble is, it's not that simple. (*She sits.*) You know, when I married you I really didn't know what I was getting into. Because of the—well, the sort of plays you write I suppose I assumed you just spend a couple of hours every morning dashing them off. It takes a lot longer than that, doesn't it?

JASON. (*A trifle bitterly.*) Yes, it takes a lot of thought to appear glib.

ALLISON. Please, Jason. Anyway, I decided I needed to find something to fill my time. Then a few weeks ago the solution presented itself. Jason, I'm pregnant.

JASON. (*Dumbfounded.*) Pregnant?

ALLISON. Two months. I put off telling you because I knew you were preoccupied and— (*She gives a small shrug.*) I thought if the play was a success we could have a double celebration. Now—well, would you accept it as a consolation prize? (*He is still staring at her. She gives a little laugh.*) Hey, I expected surprise but not catatonia.

JASON. I'm sorry. I'm very happy.

ALLISON. You *look* as if you've just lost your best friend. (*This innocent remark is not lost on him.*)

JASON. It's fatigue.

ALLISON. Maybe I shouldn't have hit you with it tonight.

JASON. No, it's—it's nice to know something I collaborated on turned out right. (*He moves to her.*) Really, I'm very pleased. (*They embrace for a moment. She looks at him.*)

ALLISON. Are we going to be all right, Jason?

JASON. (*Finally.*) Sure—we'll run for years.

ALLISON. You looked exhausted. Come to bed.

JASON. I'll—I'll be right up.

(ALLISON *exits*. PHOEBE, *her face scrubbed clean, enters*.)

PHOEBE. Did you know you're the only person I know who has monogrammed soap?

JASON. (*Distracted*.) What? Oh, when I'm not wearing clothes I'm not sure who I am.

PHOEBE. (*Notices his expression*.) Are you all right?

JASON. I'm fine. (*Briskly*.) Look, tomorrow's going to be rather hectic so let's plan on a work session at ten a.m. on Friday, okay? (*Very confused, she manages a nod*.) Good night, Phoebe. (*He exits. Totally bewildered, PHOEBE tries to fathom what has just taken place. She does this by miming what happened* before *she left the room and then what happened* after *she came back. It doesn't help and she stands in the middle of the room, completely baffled. JASON reappears in the doorway.*) Oh, I think you should know that Allison—well, she got pregnant.

PHOEBE. While I was out of the room? I'm sorry, I'm still a little—scattered.

JASON. (*Turns to exit, turns back. Awkwardly*.) Uh—if I were you—I'd pray for a girl.

PHOEBE. Why?

JASON. I'd like to name her after you.

PHOEBE. Me?

JASON. Didn't I ever tell you? I've always liked the name Phoebe.

(*They look at one another for a brief moment before he exits quickly. PHOEBE slowly moves to the coffee table, picks up the brandy snifter and tosses all the brandy down as the CURTAIN FALLS*.)

END OF ACT ONE

ACT TWO

SCENE 1

TIME: *Ten years later. A November morning in 1976.*

AT RISE: JASON, *now in his mid-forties, looking elegant in casual, expensive "work clothes," is sitting on the sofa reading some loose typewritten pages.* PHOEBE, *now in her mid-thirties, wearing a shapeless, worn jogging suit and an old baseball cap, is sitting with a sewing basket beside her, patching the knees of a child's jeans.* JASON *looks up from the pages, looks off into space, frowning.*

PHOEBE. Well?

JASON. (*Vaguely.*) It's fine.

PHOEBE. Jason, I worked six hours rewriting that scene!

JASON. (*Tosses the pages aside onto the coffee table.*) I said it was fine.

PHOEBE. You always say that when you mean "okay," "not good enough," "less than wonderful."

JASON. (*Starts to pace. Frustrated.*) It's not the scene. The scene's fine. It's the whole damned second act.

PHOEBE. So we'll change it.

JASON. I don't know, it seems like rearranging the deck chairs on the Titanic. (*He looks at her; irritably.*) Why do you wear that hat?

PHOEBE. It keeps my hair in place when I'm jogging.

JASON. It makes you look like—

PHOEBE. Katharine Hepburn.

JASON. Yogi Berra.

PHOEBE. Yes, everyone says that. What we need is—

JASON. A good rationale for him remaining faithful to his wife.

36

PHOEBE. All right. He loves her.

JASON. I mean something the audience will buy. (*He sighs, shakes his head.*) It used to be so much easier. You had a boy and girl and then you took three acts to dream them into bed together.

PHOEBE. I *still* like that story.

JASON. I mean, we must be insane! Half the world out there is doing obscene things to the other half and we're writing a play about a man who's *thinking* of cheating on his wife.

PHOEBE. People still respond to Romantic Comedies, Jason. You just have to write them differently.

JASON. (*Suddenly.*) Tell me something. Why did they take the running boards off cars?

PHOEBE. I give up.

JASON. Why did they take the elegance out of everything? Everything used to be better. Food, trains, cars, newspapers, music, hotels, movies, clothes. Everything. (*A beat.*) Maybe it's me. Maybe *I* was better.

PHOEBE. Are you depressed just because of the play?

JASON. (*Looks at her.*) Do you ever get the feeling you're living out of your times?

PHOEBE. Yes—but then I always have. Until last Thursday I wanted to be Jane Austen.

(*They are both lost in thought.* PHOEBE *with her clipboard in hand is absently wandering and making a sucking noise with her teeth.*)

JASON. I really wish you wouldn't do that.

PHOEBE. Do what?

JASON. Suck your teeth.

PHOEBE. I'm trying to think of a reason for the husband's fidelity.

JASON. So am I, but your oral hygiene isn't helping much.

(She nods thoughtfully and then suddenly falls to the floor onto her hands and goes into a series of vigorous push-ups. He absently gazes at her rear end going up and down. The double doors open and ALLISON *enters. Thirty years old, she wears a minimum of makeup with a simple hairstyle which, combined with her understated, tailored clothes, gives her the look of an attractive, capable businesswoman.* JASON *looks up.)*

JASON. Allison, can't you see we're working?

ALLISON. (*Waving a report card in her hand.*) I'm sorry, darling. I just had to tell Phoebe about Timmy's report card. (ALLISON *crosses to* PHOEBE *and hands her the report card.*)

PHOEBE. Oh, this is marvelous! I knew he could do it!

ALLISON. Well, you're the one who deserves the gold star. (*To* JASON.) Do you realize how many hours she spent tutoring Timmy? Thanks, Phoebe.

PHOEBE. Well—I like to keep my hand in. I'd better congratulate him. Where is he?

ALLISON. Outside—waiting to be congratulated.

PHOEBE. That's my boy! (*She exits.* ALLISON *watches her go as* JASON *picks up the loose pages, studies them.*)

ALLISON. Sometimes I worry about her.

JASON. Why?

ALLISON. Oh, I don't know. She doesn't seem to have much of a life.

JASON. She's one of the most successful writers in America and, since she's easily the cheapest, she's also one of the richest. (*He goes back to studying the pages.*) *I* should have her life.

ALLISON. (*Curiously.*) What does she do about sex?

JASON. (*Looks up, surprised.*) I have no idea.

ALLISON. Don't you ever ask her?

JASON. Allison, we work in here—we don't have pajama parties.

ALLISON. Oh, I know I hear a lot about the "anguish of creation," but I also hear a lot of laughter coming out of this room.

JASON. (*Regards her with some surprise.*) Are you *jealous* of Phoebe?

ALLISON. Yes, I suppose I am. I'm jealous of the on-going love affair you two have with the theatre. (*A small shrug.*) It's an obsession I can't share.

JASON. I could say that about your career in politics.

ALLISON. Oh, I'm not complaining, just stating a fact. Anyway, I just think she should be married.

JASON. (*Shrugs.*) That's her choice.

ALLISON. Not really. She's very influenced by you.

JASON. (*Looks at her.*) I *never* interfere with Phoebe's personal life.

ALLISON. Oh, come on, Jason. When that nice older man from Florida was taking her out, you said, "In five years he'll be walking around with his fly zipper not quite pulled up." That killed *that* romance.

JASON. It was just a passing observation.

ALLISON. No, you always seem able to come up with the perfect phrase to effectively eliminate anyone who gets even slightly interested in her.

JASON. What the hell are you driving at, Allison?

ALLISON. (*Evenly.*) Let her go, Jason.

JASON. Why are we talking about Phoebe?

ALLISON. Because it keeps us from talking about us, I suppose. (*They are looking at one another as* PHOEBE *enters.*)

PHOEBE. Sorry I took so long. Kate Mallory phoned. She's in town doing some P.R. for her latest movie and wants to meet with us to—quote—conceptualize the thematic problems of the play—unquote.

ALLISON. Does she really talk like that?

JASON. (*Glumly.*) She's one of those people who uses the word "artist" a lot.

ALLISON. What's she like?

PHOEBE. Well, she's a curious combination.

JASON. Mean and dumb.

PHOEBE. So how are things at City Hall?

ALLISON. Well, I wouldn't buy any municipal bonds right now. (*Checking watch.*) Which reminds me, I have a budget meeting in half an hour. (*She moves to door.*) Thanks again, Phoebe. Every working mother should have a friend like you. (*She exits.* JASON *shakes his head.*)

JASON. I married Grace Kelly and I ended up with Bella Abzug.

PHOEBE. She's a bright woman, Jason. She needed more intellectual stimulation than writing out place settings.

JASON. (*Looks up from script, regards her for a moment.*) You really *like* her, don't you?

PHOEBE. Don't you?

JASON. I have to. She's my wife.

PHOEBE. You never cheat on her.

JASON. How do you know?

PHOEBE. Because when you're not with her, you're with me. Why don't you?

JASON. I'm not allowed. I believe it's one of the most important rules.

PHOEBE. That's not good enough, Jason.

JASON. I hate it when you lapse back into schoolmarmish-ness. (*She doesn't say anything.*) All right. A few years ago I owned a delicate China teapot. One day I dropped it and it split right down the middle. Well, I glued it together and it looked as if it had never been broken. Then a few months later, for no apparent reason, it suddenly exploded into a thousand pieces. I suppose what I'm trying to say is that, despite all appearances, it's better to keep your teapot intact.

(PHOEBE, *furiously writing what* JASON *has been saying, crosses back to her chair Stage Right. When she is finished writing . . .*)

PHOEBE. That's sweet.

JASON. Yes, I thought you'd buy that. (PHOEBE *puts her clipboard down and picks up a small cassette recorder and starts it. We hear the strains of BUT NOT FOR ME played in a lush instrumental version.*) Do you have to play that music?

PHOEBE. (*Absently.*) It's the perfect mood music for writing this play.

JASON. But you've been playing it for six months now. I mean it's really getting on my nerves.

PHOEBE. What makes the husband suddenly fall in love with his wife again?

JASON. (*Muttering.*) Pity we can't use the Cinderella convention.

PHOEBE. You mean where the girl takes off her glasses, lets down her hair and he realizes she's beautiful.

JASON. Don't laugh. Audiences used to love it.

PHOEBE. You think someone can fall in love that fast.

JASON. Of course. Even happened to me once. (*Surprised, she looks at him.*) It was at the Tony Awards a couple of years ago. I saw this woman from the back. She was wearing a blue taffeta dress and had gleaming blonde hair that cascaded down over creamy white shoulders. I fell instantly in love and remained that way for about five seconds. (*A shrug—casually.*) Then she turned around and it was you.

PHOEBE. (*Flustered.*) Yes—well—you're right. I mean, I don't believe we can get away with Pygmalion anymore. (*We hear the front DOORBELL RING.*)

JASON. Who the hell can that be?

PHOEBE. Probably Leo Janowitz.

JASON. My God, he's been hanging around for three weeks. Doesn't he have a story by now?

PHOEBE. I thought you found him amusing.

JASON. That doesn't mean I want to adopt him.

PHOEBE. It was green actually.

JASON. Green?

PHOEBE. The dress. It was from the second scene of "Somewhere Every Summer." I borrowed it from wardrobe.

JASON. I might have known you wouldn't have bought it.

(*The door opens and* LEO JANOWITZ *enters. In his mid-thirties, has unruly hair, is dressed in a rumpled suit, and has a serious, reserved demeanor that almost masks a very dry sense of humor. His speech has the rough edges of the street and he tends to cut through to the core of things. He carries a small notebook and pencil.*)

LEO. (*Without preamble—checking notes.*) I know you're busy but I just wanted to check some facts. What year did you graduate from Yale?

JASON. Look, I'd prefer that you didn't mention I went to Yale.

LEO. Bad school?

JASON. I don't like anything published about my background that could cause people to pigeonhole me.

LEO. I don't get it.

PHOEBE. I think Jason means he would rather be judged by his work alone.

LEO. Yeah?

JASON. Have you seen any of my plays?

LEO. Nope. Read 'em all.

JASON. (*Waits for the compliment. There is only a pause.*) Look, there's one thing you should know—I'm not offended by flattery.

LEO. I don't know anything about the theatre.

JASON. Then why were you given this piece to write?

LEO. It's a fill-in assignment until I can get back to my serious stuff.

PHOEBE. (*Quickly.*) Leo just got back from two years in Russia.

JASON. You're an expert on Russia?

LEO. Yeah—well, I speak the lingo.

JASON. How many other "lingoes" do you speak?

LEO. A few.

JASON. You mind if *I* ask a question? (LEO *shrugs*.) I suspect that underneath that unkempt exterior you're an educated, civilized man. Why do you go to all that trouble to hide it with bad tailoring?

LEO. It's no trouble.

JASON. (*Moving to door*.) Is that all?

LEO. Just one more thing. (*Checking notebook*.) What's your biggest regret?

JASON. That Americans can't be knighted. (*He exits*.)

LEO. Miss Craddock?

PHOEBE. (*Crossing to him*.) Yes? (LEO *grabs her and kisses her*.) Please, Leo—Jason could come back in.

LEO. So? He's not your father.

PHOEBE. (*Moving away*.) Well, he is in a way.

LEO. Professionally?

PHOEBE. Every way. A writing collaboration is a very intimate relationship.

LEO. Yeah, I been meaning to ask you about that.

PHOEBE. (*Looks at him*.) This for the article?

LEO. I've already written the article. I wanted an excuse to see you.

PHOEBE. Why?

LEO. I got the hots for you.

PHOEBE. (*Flustered*.) Yes—well, I'm sorry you caught us at such a busy time.

LEO. Is it just that you've never learned to accept a compliment or do you really believe as a woman you're the pits? Every time I get personal, you change the subject.

PHOEBE. I'm sorry. (*Blushing*.) I'm just not used to such—an overt response to my—girlish charms.

LEO. I want you to marry me, Phoebe.

PHOEBE. (*Stares at him*.) Are you serious?

LEO. Yes. (*She stares at him blankly.*) What's the matter? Am I being too overt?

PHOEBE. (*Sitting.*) No, I—I just need a moment to absorb this.

LEO. Okay. (*He waits.*) Absorbed it yet? (*She manages a nod.*) So about Jason. You been to bed with him?

PHOEBE. Why—why would you even think that?

LEO. I'm a pragmatist. You're out of town together. It's an old axiom—desire plus opportunity usually equals humpage. Am I being too personal?

PHOEBE. Yes—you are.

LEO. There's a reason. I've been assigned to the Paris bureau. I leave in five weeks and I want to take you with me. The point is, I can't stick around until the third act to see who gets the girl.

PHOEBE. I see.

LEO. So—you have sex together?

PHOEBE. Once. Well, not together.

LEO. (*Finally.*) That's some trick.

PHOEBE. (*Embarrassed.*) I mean it was once for me. None for Jason— (*He is staring at her.*) It's hard to explain. We were out of town with a show—in Chicago—and the play wasn't working—it never did work—we still don't know why. Anyway, we'd rewritten half the script, but it hadn't helped at all and we just didn't know how to fix it. One night we got back to the hotel, exhausted, our brains numb—totally depressed. We started to drink and Jason became quite drunk—and then—more out of frustration, I suppose—I don't know—he started to—to make love to me, but—right in the middle—he passed out.

LEO. In the middle?

PHOEBE. Well, if we're going to be technical, a third of the way through. It could have been a quarter. I'm only guessing, of course—I mean I have no means of comparison—with Jason, that is. (*She clears her throat.*) When I woke up, he was gone.

LEO. Then what happened?

PHOEBE. That's it.

LEO. You never discussed it?

PHOEBE. Jason obviously didn't remember—or if he did—he didn't want to.

LEO. Are you in love with him, Phoebe?

PHOEBE. I was.

LEO. And now?

PHOEBE. Now we just write plays together.

LEO. So will you marry me? (*He holds up his hand.*) Before you say anything you should know there are three answers.

PHOEBE. Three?

LEO. "Yes"—"No"—or "Let's talk about it some more." (*As she opens her mouth to speak.*) But first— something to help you make up your mind. I love you, Phoebe. (*He kisses her. JASON enters now attired in an elegant suit. He stops, completely stunned by what he sees. After a moment, sensing that someone else is in the room, PHOEBE and LEO break apart. PHOEBE is very embarrassed but LEO is totally unflustered and casually notes JASON's new wardrobe.*) You look as if you're going somewhere important.

JASON. I am. My tailor's. (*He moves to desk, busies himself with some papers.*) But we have to finish some work first.

LEO. (*Pleasantly.*) Okay, I don't have to be hit by a truck. (*To PHOEBE.*) I'll be in touch, huh? (*She manages a nod and LEO exits. JASON is still making a great show of studying the script pages.*)

PHOEBE. (*Finally.*) You don't really want to work, do you?

JASON. Why do you say that?

PHOEBE. You never like to sit down and get creases before you visit your tailor.

JASON. (*Still studying script—overly casual.*) Do you mind telling me why he was doing that?

PHOEBE. He finds me attractive.

JASON. Oh, come on, Phoebe! You expect me to buy that? (*She can't think of a reply to this.*) I mean, you must have done something to bring it on.

PHOEBE. You make it sound like a migraine headache.

JASON. (*Impatiently.*) Are you trying to tell me that the first time he's left alone with you, he's overcome with desire and leaps on you?

PHOEBE. Of course not. We've been—seeing each other.

JASON. He's been interviewing you at night?

PHOEBE. No, it wasn't a professional thing. They were more—do they still call them "dates"?

JASON. (*Sitting.*) This is no time to be coy!

PHOEBE. (*Puzzled.*) Why are you so upset?

JASON. (*Thrown.*) Upset?

PHOEBE. You just sat down and creased yourself.

JASON. Well, naturally, I'm somewhat alarmed.

PHOEBE. Why?

JASON. (*On his feet again.*) You know, for someone so talented you can be remarkably obtuse! Don't you know anything?

PHOEBE. Now you're shouting.

JASON. Because you should know better! He's a *journalist!* He's a person who makes a living writing down what people say when they're off guard.

PHOEBE. We didn't discuss my work. We just—hung out together.

JASON. Hung out? Aren't you getting a little old for that sort of thing?

PHOEBE. I wish I could think of an answer to that, but right now I'm in the middle of a hot flash.

JASON. Are you trying to tell me this is a *romantic* relationship?

PHOEBE. I'm not trying to tell you anything. Jason, what is the *matter* with you?

JASON. I don't want to see you get hurt and depressed.

PHOEBE. Oh?

JASON. Yes, you know how difficult it is for you to be funny when you're depressed.

PHOEBE. I don't have any illusions about the way Leo feels about me.

JASON. (*Looks at her, relaxes somewhat.*) Good.

PHOEBE. (*Rather enjoying herself.*) He wants to marry me.

JASON. (*Is absolutely floored. Finally.*) How do you know?

PHOEBE. He asked me.

JASON. When?

PHOEBE. Just now.

JASON. (*Incredulous.*) While you were wearing that hat?

PHOEBE. Maybe he's a Yogi Berra fan.

JASON. I want you to stop seeing him.

PHOEBE. Why?

JASON. (*Looks at her.*) Do I really have to say it? You want me to spell it out for you?

PHOEBE. (*Finally.*) I'm not sure.

JASON. (*Avoiding her eyes.*) No, perhaps it *is* time we stopped skirting the issue. We're going to have to deal with it sometime. Better now than when it's too late. (*He looks at her, takes a breath.*) Phoebe, our second act doesn't work at all! (PHOEBE *just stares at him, turns and exits. Looking Stage Right at* PHOEBE'S *chair.*) Leo's the sort of man who wears his bowling shirt when he's not bowling. He's a lot like Jimmy Breslin—but without the polish. If they made triple-knit suits, Leo would wear them. (*The CURTAIN FALLS.*)

END OF SCENE 1, ACT TWO

ACT TWO

SCENE 2

THE TIME: *Late afternoon, five weeks later.*

AT RISE: *The Stage is empty. The double doors open and*

BLANCHE *and* PHOEBE *enter. They take off their coats and other winter paraphernalia during following.*

PHOEBE. I hope nothing's happened to him.

BLANCHE. It's not like Jason not to keep an appointment. When was the last time you saw him?

PHOEBE. About two o'clock. He stormed out of rehearsals when the actors started improvising.

BLANCHE. Maybe he went to beat up on Lee Strasberg.

PHOEBE. (*Moves to dressing room entrance. Calling.*) Jason! Jason, are you here? (*There is a slight pause.*)

JASON. (*Offstage.*) Yes, what is it?

PHOEBE. Are you all right?

JASON. (*Offstage.*) Of course. I'll—I'll be right out. (PHOEBE *and* BLANCHE *take off their coats.*)

BLANCHE. How are rehearsals going?

PHOEBE. Well, the leading man's a bit wooden.

BLANCHE. A bit wooden? The man's a talking tree! What else?

PHOEBE. Jason and Kate Mallory loathe each other.

BLANCHE. I'm on his side.

PHOEBE. Oh, I know she's impossible, but I really do think he's overreacting.

BLANCHE. What changes does she want?

PHOEBE. The same one. Beware of people with few ideas, Blanche. They cling to them with such tenacity.

BLANCHE. She still wants you to rewrite the ending?

PHOEBE. She doesn't want her character to go back to her husband. She's got this idea in her head that she's the Joan of Arc of the Seventies and keeps saying, ''Why should I end up with any man? Why can't I go off and make a life of my own?''

BLANCHE. How about you, my love? You look harassed.

PHOEBE. That's funny. I *feel* suicidal.

BLANCHE. Are you going to marry that nice young man?

PHOEBE. Well, I've gone from ''no'' to ''perhaps''—but I'm not fooling anybody—not even me.

BLANCHE. Isn't he leaving for Paris in a couple of days?

PHOEBE. Oh, it's impossible, Blanche! Even if I wanted to get married, I can't walk out on Jason now.

BLANCHE. He'd survive. (*Surprised,* PHOEBE *looks at her.*) Oh, he'd scream bloody murder, but he'd survive.

PHOEBE. I take it this is my friend not my agent talking.

BLANCHE. (*Shrugs.*) I'd just hate to see you turn into one of those dotty women writers who drink too much and wear hats.

JASON. (*Enters from his dressing room and crosses directly to his desk.*) Pour me a double, will you, Blanche?

BLANCHE. Have you been eavesdropping?

JASON. Of course not. Who can hear anything over the clash of your bracelets?

BLANCHE. What are you doing back here anyway? You were supposed to meet us at Sardi's.

JASON. Yes—well, something came up. (*At this point,* KATE MALLORY *enters from the dressing room. She is a soft, pretty woman in her late thirties with a deceptively gentle, feminine manner and sweet smile. She has absolutely no sense of humor. The two women look at her in surprise. This surprise gradually changes to puzzlement, because, although fully clothed, there is something slightly "off" about* KATE's *appearance. We and they will realize that she is wearing her dress inside out.* KATE *never becomes aware of this.*) Uh—Kate and I decided that our differences were undermining the—uh, creative process, so I invited her over so we could discuss our problems frankly and arrive at a reasonable solution.

KATE. And, of course—as always happens when two human beings reach out to one another—it worked.

JASON. The point is, we discovered that we're both after the same thing—the best possible production. We've just been coming at it from two different places.

KATE. (*Notices* PHOEBE *peering at her in a dazed manner.*) Is there something the matter?

PHOEBE. What? Uh, no.

KATE. I sense some bad vibes in the room.

BLANCHE. It's probably the radiator.

JASON. Would you care for a drink?

KATE. No, thanks. I stopped four years ago when I woke up in a motel room with those four jockeys and the Vice President. (*There is a pause.*)

BLANCHE. (*Finally.*) Who were the jockeys? (*The other three turn to look at her. She shrugs.*) I'm not political.

(KATE *moves Downstage for her coat revealing a fairly large label on the back of her dress. Now even* JASON *is aware of the way she is dressed.*)

KATE. I can't seem to find my coat. (*She turns, notices the other three staring at her.*) Why is everyone staring at me?

BLANCHE. (*Finally.*) Star quality?

JASON. (*Picks up her coat, quickly moves to her, holds it up for her to put on.*) Here's your coat.

KATE. I'll carry it, thanks. Should I call a cab or can someone give me a lift?

BLANCHE. My car's outside. Where can I drop you?

KATE. At the park. I'll walk the rest of the way.

BLANCHE. (*Moves to get her coat. Just making conversation.*) Are you enjoying your stay?

KATE. (*With a sweet smile.*) Oh, I just love New York. Every time I come here, I feel like going down on the whole city. (*There is a moment's embarrassed pause.*)

BLANCHE. Well, you certainly have the weather for it. Your visit I mean. (*A beat.*)

KATE. I want you to know a beautiful thing happened this afternoon. Two human beings made contact. Now let's go to work!

(*She exits.* BLANCHE *shoots an incredulous look at the still stunned* PHOEBE *and exits. There is a small, tense pause.*)

JASON. Yes—well— (*Avoiding her eyes, he moves briskly to the desk and picks up some script pages.*) We need to take ten minutes out of the play. Nothing in life should last longer than two hours. (PHOEBE, *who hasn't moved, clears her throat.*) We also need a new curtain line for scene four. You have any ideas? (*She doesn't answer, but clears her throat and stares straight ahead.*) Phoebe, are you going to stand there making raspy, little noises or are we going to work?

PHOEBE. (*Tightly—a touch of the school-teacher.*) It's no good you know.

JASON. What isn't?

PHOEBE. We all noticed, Jason. That woman had her dress inside out.

JASON. (*Flustered.*) So, she's sloppy. You should be able to identify with that.

PHOEBE. Her label was showing!

JASON. (*Uncomfortably.*) Phoebe, we have a lot of work to do here.

PHOEBE. (*In a dry, strained voice.*) You went to bed with her, didn't you?

JASON. You want me to stand up and share it with the rest of the class?

PHOEBE. Don't deny it.

JASON. Look, do you want to fix this play or not?

PHOEBE. (*Stares at him, absolutely stunned, her worst fears confirmed.*) My God, how *could* you!!

JASON. Well—it wasn't easy. (*She is staring at him, her eyes welling up with tears.*) Phoebe, I didn't commit an axe murder! Why are you staring at me like that?

PHOEBE. It's—it's so—unprofessional!

JASON. Actually, it was *very* professional.

PHOEBE. (*Tightly—moving away.*) Well, I'm glad she has some technique *somewhere*.

JASON. What I mean was it *started* out as a professional thing. (*A trifle desperately.*) Look, I did it for you too.

PHOEBE. (*Icily.*) Did I enjoy it?

JASON. I was just trying to—improve my relationship with her.

PHOEBE. (*Exploding.*) Oh, don't try to romanticize it! You've been *cheating!!* You committed adultery!

JASON. (*Stares at her.*) You know, I don't believe this. You sound like a *wife.*

PHOEBE. (*Still angry but flustered.*) I happen to be a friend of your wife.

JASON. It's not the same thing.

PHOEBE. I'm your partner!

JASON. Exactly. You're not my priest, you're not even my mistress—and my private life is none of your business.

PHOEBE. I don't care what you do in your private life, but—but you did it right here—in our *office*—where we *work!*

JASON. Phoebe, it's not a cathedral. Now what the hell is the matter with you?

PHOEBE. I thought I was working with a man of honor.

JASON. Did I ever say or do one thing to make you believe that?

PHOEBE. You said you wanted to keep your teapot intact!!

JASON. Oh, for God's sake—you sound just like a woman.

PHOEBE. (*Tightly.*) It's one of my best impressions.

JASON. Yes, that's always been the problem. (*She looks at him.*) Well, if you were a man you wouldn't be carrying on like this. We wouldn't even be *talking* about it. At least not in the same way. (*She doesn't say anything.*) We'd have a couple of laughs and forget it. You'd cover for me. You'd be a pal—a buddy.

PHOEBE. (*Finally.*) I find that—revolting.

JASON. Look, what exactly would you like me to say?

PHOEBE. I'm trying—very hard—to understand your actions. (*A beat.*) Do you love her?

JASON. (*Incredulously.*) Love her? I can't even hear her from the balcony!

PHOEBE. Then *why?*

JASON. Oh, for God's sake, don't you understand *anything* about sex?

PHOEBE. Evidently not. (*She is having trouble controlling her tears and moves to get her coat.*)

JASON. What are you doing?

PHOEBE. Leaving.

JASON. All right, I know it's been a long day. (*He sits with pages of script.*) I'll work on the cuts and tomorrow we can concentrate on the—

PHOEBE. I mean permanently. (*He looks at her as she puts on hat, gloves and scarf.*)

JASON. Are you serious? (*She doesn't answer.*) You'd actually walk out on a ten-year partnership over something so stupid and trivial as this?

PHOEBE. (*In a strange voice.*) Goodbye, Jason. (*She moves towards the door and opens it. Just as she is about to exit,* JASON, *not looking at her, speaks quietly.*)

JASON. Did you know I had my nose fixed? (*She stops. Finally, her curiosity gets the better of her. She turns.*)

PHOEBE. What?

JASON. My nose. It's fixed. I had it done years ago.

PHOEBE. (*Bewildered.*) What has that to do with—

JASON. I'm trying to explain why this afternoon happened.

PHOEBE. (*Baffled.*) She found out and blackmailed you into going to bed with her?

JASON. My teeth are capped, too.

PHOEBE. I really don't understand why—*all* of them?

JASON. (*Irritably.*) No, not all of them! Look, will you stop interrupting? I'm trying to make a point. Please sit down, and hear me out. After ten years, you at least owe me that. (*After a moment, she sits and waits.* JASON *closes door and starts speaking, not looking at her.*) My real name isn't Jason Carmichael. It's Joey Mahovalich. I didn't graduate from Yale—I never even finished high school. I grew up, a fat little kid with a bad nose and a worse accent on 12th

Street in the South Side of Detroit. Did you ever notice I have no relatives? My father wasn't a lawyer—he worked for the Gas Company. I never knew him—he ran off with a woman who lived upstairs when I was four years old. My mother took a job in the cafeteria at the G.M. plant so I lived pretty much on the streets. She died when I was thirteen and I was put in a series of foster homes. I was arrested three times before I was fifteen for stealing—mostly food from vending machines. (*He looks at her.*) Do you know who I really am?

PHOEBE. Oliver Twist? (*He doesn't smile. She makes a gesture of "forget that."*)

JASON. I'm a totally manufactured man. I didn't like my life, hated what I was—so I became someone else. You know why I married Allison? I couldn't get over the fact that a girl with her background would want someone like *me*. But she did. My God, now I had the "right" wife. So there I was—the successful, urbane playwright—the host of the most glittering dinner parties in town. Fooled a lot of people; but *I* never believed it. Inside the Saville Row suits there was always the ugly, fat little kid waiting to be found out. So much for the past. Lately, I've been feeling more—unattractive than usual. Things between Allison and I haven't been—Look, I'll be forty-six next month. Middle age. Pick your cliché. (*She remains silent, her face impassive. Finally:*) And none of that is the real reason this happened. I was angry at you—because of Leo. I suppose—in some way—I wanted to lash back. (*She is too astounded to say anything. A pause.*) All right. I was terrified of losing you. So you see before you an insecure, middle-aged man who just this afternoon made a complete ass of himself and couldn't regret it more.

PHOEBE. They did an incredible job on your nose.

JASON. Is that all you have to say?

PHOEBE. Look, you've given me some understanding of why you did what you did. But, right now, I'm still not too fond of you.

JASON. Well, that makes two of us.

PHOEBE. (*Takes her hat, gloves and scarf off and picks up the script he has been working on from the coffee table.*) I think you may have cut too deeply here. The last line contains the right set up for the Act One curtain line.

JASON. Is class dismissed Miss Craddock? I've been thinking about the end of the play. I think I have the solution.

PHOEBE. Good. Now all we have to do is come up with the problem.

JASON. Phoebe, it's all too neat, too slick. You know what I mean?

PHOEBE. Yes. Professional.

JASON. Pat.

PHOEBE. (*Warily.*) What do you have in mind?

JASON. Well, it's not clearly formulated in my mind yet—I'm just thinking out loud—but supposing she doesn't stay with the lover *or* return to her husband?

PHOEBE. That only leaves the seventy-five-year-old gardener.

JASON. (*Doing a very good acting job.*) I don't know—I just have a gut feeling about it. Wait a minute—why does she have to end up with anyone? I mean this is 1975. It'll give it a more contemporary feeling.

PHOEBE. You mean ''make her a Joan of Arc of the seventies.''

JASON. What a good idea. (PHOEBE *throws the script at* JASON, *exits briefly to the dressing room and returns with a battered suitcase. She throws it on the ground, opens it.*) What are you doing?

PHOEBE. Packing!

JASON. Because you don't like my idea for a second act? (*Falsely jolly.*) Really, a simple ''no'' would be sufficient.

(*During the following scene* PHOEBE *gets various articles from around the room and throws them into the case. The articles include a portable typewriter, a number of*

*books, scripts, assorted objects from the desk drawers,
jogging suit, baseball hat, etc. Her "packing" is noisy
and punctuates some of her remarks.)*

PHOEBE. No, it wouldn't.

JASON. Oh, come on, Phoebe. You've lost all sense of
proportion.

PHOEBE. (*Exploding.*) And you've lost your integrity!!
You've sold out to that woman!!

JASON. *One* sell-out and I've lost my integrity? Look, do
you know what you're doing?

PHOEBE. I'm getting married, going to Paris, and having
three children.

JASON. But you can't leave right now! We have a play in
rehearsal!

PHOEBE. Send me the reviews.

JASON. That's not good enough, damn it! You have re-
sponsibilities here.

PHOEBE. I'm sure you and Kate Mallory can take care of
any rewrites.

JASON. I'm not talking about the play. What about the
children?

PHOEBE. I'm not their mother.

JASON. You're more than their mother. You *like* them.
You listen to them.

PHOEBE. Well, maybe if you'd been the father you
should I wouldn't have had to spend so much time with
them.

JASON. Wait a minute—there has to be more to this than
an artistic difference of opinion. Just what is bothering you,
Phoebe?

PHOEBE. (*Stops packing, looks at him.*) Bothering me?
All right, I'll tell you what's 'bothering' me. I don't like
you anymore! You're a vain, arrogant, insensitive, selfish
bully!

JASON. I am not vain!

PHOEBE. (*Stabs a finger in the direction of the sofa.*) Then why do you always sit on that couch? (JASON *is nonplussed.*) You know why: So you can look at yourself all day in— (*Pointing at mirror.*) *That* mirror! I think you're about to get an idea but you're *admiring* yourself!

JASON. (*Coldly.*) Is that all?

PHOEBE. No, it's not all. Whenever we eat in a restaurant you always take the best seat with your back to the wall so everyone can see you!

JASON. And so they can't see you! You dress like a walking garage sale!

PHOEBE. (*She moves to bookshelf to get book.*) My father has a word for people like you—"jerk"!

JASON. I see your gift for language runs in the family.

PHOEBE. You said you liked my father.

JASON. I lied. Your father is a boring, illiterate, old poop! (*Pointing at book she is holding.*) Wait a minute—that was given to both of us!

PHOEBE. It was given to me!

JASON. Read the inscription!

PHOEBE. Oh, keep the damn book! (*She throws it at him and it hits him in the chest.*)

JASON. You could have broken a rib! I mean just who do you think you are?

PHOEBE. (*Hysterically.*) I'll tell you who I am! You're full of shit—that's who I am! (*He is too astounded to reply. She goes back to packing.*) God, I'll be so glad not to have to face you every day!

JASON. (*Angered.*) You think it's been easy living with your relentless perkiness all these years? Have you any idea how depressing it is to be around that much—niceness?

PHOEBE. (*Thrown.*) Niceness is depressing?

JASON. Mealy-mouthed niceness! Like that time when that actress propositioned you. She asked, "Are you gay?" and do you know what you said?

PHOEBE. (*Puzzled.*) I said, "No, I'm not."

JASON. No, you didn't. You said, "No, I'm not—*but thank you for asking*"!! (*At this point* ALLISON *enters but stops when she sees what is going on. Neither* JASON *nor* PHOEBE *notices her.*) You're afraid of offending anyone!

PHOEBE. Yes, well, maybe that's why I say "goodbye" when I leave a room and "hello" when I come in.

JASON. Very original.

PHOEBE. You *never* say "hello" or "goodbye." You just leave. It's the ultimate conceit!

JASON. Better than your stammering, blushing humble act. Let me tell you something—you're not talented enough to be that humble!

(*At this point he notices* ALLISON. PHOEBE *also turns and looks at her. They watch her as she tiptoes across the room, picks up some mending from* PHOEBE's *corner Downstage Right. She tiptoes back to the door.*)

ALLISON. I'm sorry. I didn't realize you were working. (ALLISON *exits.* PHOEBE *picks up a staple gun, holds it up.*)

PHOEBE. This is mine.

JASON. (*Moves to the desk.*) Here, you want to take some paper? You want half the pencils? (*Throwing objects from the desk.*) Paper clips? Used typewriter ribbons? Wait a minute—there's half a box of Kleenex in the dressing room!

PHOEBE. I'm walking out of here with exactly what I came in with!

JASON. Plus fifty percent of my royalties!

PHOEBE. Which I more than earned!!

JASON. And from which you have the first nickel—plus towels and soap from every hotel we ever stayed in. You know what I really despise about you? I loathe your—

PHOEBE. Cheapness.

JASON. Your finishing my sentences for me!

PHOEBE. *Someone* has to do it!

JASON. (*Infuriated.*) You really want to know what I've always really hated about you?

PHOEBE. Why not? You've gone this far.

JASON. I've always hated your ass!

PHOEBE. Eloquent. Very eloquent.

JASON. I mean, I *literally hate your ass!!* You and your damned exercises! Every morning for ten years I turn around and find I'm addressing your rear end. Believe me, it's not a pretty sight.

PHOEBE. (*Hurt—fighting back the tears.*) Yes—well—I think I'll get a second opinion on that. Goodbye, Jason.

JASON. Phoebe, you can't leave. (*A last desperate plea.*) I named one of my children after you!

PHOEBE. (*Finally—quietly.*) It's not enough, Jason. (*She goes to close the suitcase but it is so loaded it won't close. In a mixture of frustration and rage, she kicks the case.*) Oh, to hell with it! (PHOEBE *takes a small tank of goldfish under her arm and crosses to the door.*)

JASON. It won't last three months! Once he sees those substandard flannel nightgowns he'll run for the nearest fire escape! (*This really stings her. She turns around.*)

PHOEBE. (*With dignity.*) I only have one reply to that. Even an egg takes three minutes.

JASON. (*Baffled.*) What?

PHOEBE. (*Tearfully yelling.*) You were inadequate in Chicago!!

(*She slams out the door leaving an outraged* JASON. *He crosses to the overstuffed suitcase and kicks it violently. It flies open and the impact has jolted the tape recorder and the music of "BUT NOT FOR ME" fills the room. The anger drains out of* JASON *as he lifts the recorder out of the debris. He puts the recorder down when he notices her red baseball cap on the top of all the junk. He picks it up, crosses slowly to the sofa, finally puts on the cap and sits dejectedly.*)

JASON. Oh, Phoebe—you always were such a sloppy sentimentalist. (*The CURTAIN FALLS.*)

END OF ACT TWO

ACT THREE

SCENE 1

THE TIME: *Two years later. A mid-September morning.*

AT RISE: *The Stage is empty. The room looks as if it hasn't been cleaned in weeks and is littered with old newspapers, magazines, dirty shirts, some jackets and trousers thrown haphazardly over chairs, paper coffee cups. The desk and tables are piled with scripts and mail, mostly unopened.* BLANCHE, *dressed for fall, and carrying some containers of sendout food, enters, surveys the room with distaste.*

BLANCHE. (*Calling.*) Jason! Jason, it's Blanche! Jason, I brought you some hot food! Jason!

(JASON, *unshaven, wearing some wrinkled trousers, shirt, and an old, woolen cardigan, and looking very much the worse for wear, enters from the dressing room.*)

JASON. (*Quietly.*) Blanche, you're not in the Follies anymore. You don't have to be heard at the back of the house.

BLANCHE. (*Looks at him.*) You know if you expect your social life to pick up, you've gotta keep the phone on the hook. (*He moves to bar. She picks up the phone and puts it back on the desk.*) God, you look awful. Have you seen a doctor lately? I mean, you really look unhealthy.

JASON. Look, will you stop reviewing me if I give you a drink?

BLANCHE. It's only eleven a.m.

JASON. I have a watch, Blanche. (*He pours himself a drink as she clears a space for food cartons during following.*)

61

BLANCHE. I don't know how you can live in this mess. Don't you ever have a cleaning woman?

JASON. A cleaning woman? Listen, I can barely afford to keep the Bentley.

BLANCHE. I still don't understand why you don't sell this place or at least rent out the two top floors.

JASON. Blanche, I'm simply going through a dry spell— I'm not quite ready to open a boarding house yet.

BLANCHE. Two years isn't a dry spell—it's retirement.

JASON. I've had a few distractions.

BLANCHE. Okay, you were upset when Phoebe left—I can understand that. I could even understand when you were divorced and didn't draw a sober breath for a year. What I don't understand is why you and the typewriter have become natural enemies.

JASON. (*Looks at her, sighs.*) I tried, my love. Believe me, I tried but— (*He shakes head.*) it's just—too damned hard.

BLANCHE. You don't even read the scripts I send you. You know that last play was by a young writer who's had three off-Broadway productions that got very good reviews.

JASON. (*Mildly.*) Blanche, just because he's never had a commercial success doesn't necessarily mean he's talented.

BLANCHE. (*Looks at him for a moment.*) Why did you tell that man from CBS you'd only write for TV if your children got rickets?

JASON. I was trying to let him down easily.

BLANCHE. (*Hands him a carton of soup.*) Here, drink this soup. (*She watches him as he gingerly tastes soup.*) Have you read Phoebe's novel yet?

JASON. Novel?

BLANCHE. Oh, come on, Jason—it's been on the best seller list for weeks. Five major studios are falling over themselves trying to buy the movie rights.

JASON. Please, I'm trying to eat. If you don't mind, I'd

rather not listen to the dubious accomplishments of a woman who ruined my life.

BLANCHE. What did Phoebe ever do to you?

JASON. She's a literary opportunist. She drained me dry and then she left me.

BLANCHE. (*Incredulous.*) She got married.

JASON. Exactly. You don't get married and then have a best seller suddenly pop out of your head. She must have been hoarding the idea all the time we were partners. That's like a wife secretly siphoning off your money into a Swiss bank account.

BLANCHE. You said she ruined your life.

JASON. She caused my divorce.

BLANCHE. (*Surprised.*) How?

JASON. (*Looks at her.*) For that you'll have to wait for my memoirs.

BLANCHE. She's back in town.

JASON. Who cares?

BLANCHE. They arrived three days ago. Leo managed to get himself assigned back here so Phoebe could publicize her book.

JASON. How is she?

BLANCHE. You can see for yourself. She's due here any moment.

JASON. (*Alarmed.*) I don't want to see her. I'm not ready for that yet.

BLANCHE. When will you be ready?

JASON. When I have three hits running on Broadway. (*He picks up phone, holds up receiver.*) Here—you'd better stop her.

BLANCHE. Why?

JASON. (*Impatiently.*) Because I don't want her to see me like this with my hair in curlers wearing a cheap kimono! (BLANCHE *hasn't moved. He puts the receiver down on the desk and moves to get his raincoat.*) Anyway, I have appointments all day.

BLANCHE. Will you take some advice from an old broad who loves you like a mother? (*He looks at her.*) When you see her, don't put on airs. You're much more appealing when you're vulnerable.

(*He grabs raincoat and starts for the door but stops as* PHOEBE *enters. She is impeccably groomed and coiffured and looks absolutely stunning in a chic, designer suit. Her manner has also changed and she projects an image of confident sophistication. They look at one another for a long moment.*)

PHOEBE. (*Finally.*) Hello, Jason.

JASON. Hello. (*There is a pause. She looks around the room.*)

PHOEBE. I see you've redecorated.

JASON. I see you have, too.

PHOEBE. Oh, I took off my glasses and let down my hair. Works every time. (*She is looking at him, trying to hide her surprise at his appearance.*)

JASON. I know. I look awful.

PHOEBE. (*Easily.*) I wouldn't say that.

JASON. Neither would I, actually. Blanche said it.

BLANCHE. Well, look at him. His skin has an unhealthy pallor, his face is all rumpled and I'm sure his liver is the size of the Palladium.

JASON. Nothing left but to shoot me. (*As* BLANCHE *heads for door, panicky at being left alone with* PHOEBE.) Where are you going?

BLANCHE. To make some coffee.

JASON. Oh, sit down. You don't even know your way to the kitchen.

BLANCHE. It's easy. I just keep walking until the floor gets hard and cold and if I look up and see a lot of white furniture, that's it. (*She exits. There is an awkward pause.*)

JASON. How's Leo?

PHOEBE. Fine. He's out apartment hunting right now. (JASON *nods*.) Oh, Timmy and little Phoebe send their love.

JASON. You saw them?

PHOEBE. We drove up to Tarrytown for the weekend.

JASON. How's Allison?

PHOEBE. Very well. I suppose you know she's running for Congress. (*He nods. A small pause.*) You live alone?

JASON. All alone. (*A small pause.*)

PHOEBE. I'm sorry I walked out on you, Jason. I mean at that time—in the middle of a production.

JASON. It wouldn't have made any difference if you'd stayed. Nothing could have helped that play. (*He frowns.*) And, since we're on that subject, I said a lot of things in the heat of anger before you left that—

PHOEBE. You don't have to apologize for—

JASON. No, no—there's something I said that's really been bothering me and I'd like to retract it. It was stupid and childish and I should never have said it.

PHOEBE. What?

JASON. I never had my nose fixed.

PHOEBE. I know.

JASON. How?

PHOEBE. It was out of character.

JASON. For me to have it done?

PHOEBE. No, for you to admit it.

JASON. (*Gives her a wintry smile.*) I'd forgotten what an excellent judge of character you were.

PHOEBE. Why are you nursing such a grudge?

JASON. (*Turns to face her.*) You're asking that seriously?

PHOEBE. It's rather important we clear the air.

JASON. Why?

PHOEBE. You'll understand later. All right, I admit I left you at an inopportune time—but is that any reason to go into a childish sulk?

JASON. Childish? You turned my life upside down, you ruined my marriage!

PHOEBE. (*Puzzled.*) How did I ruin your marriage?

JASON. (*Evasively.*) Look, I really don't see any point in rehashing all this.

PHOEBE. In what way did I ruin your marriage?

JASON. All right! Do you know why Allison left me?

PHOEBE. She found out about you and Kate Mallory.

JASON. And how do you think she found out? Why do you think she kept her nose to the scent like a Tennessee bloodhound?

PHOEBE. I have no idea.

JASON. Allison kept asking me why you'd walked out and wouldn't accept any of the reasons I gave her. It was maddening. She said for you to leave me I must have done something absolutely horrendous.

PHOEBE. Why did she think that?

JASON. Look, she was quite demented at the time— totally irrational—it made no sense at all.

PHOEBE. What didn't?

JASON. She said that all the years you and I were together you'd been in love with me.

PHOEBE. I was in love with you.

JASON. Well—now you can see why I bear you a certain—animosity.

PHOEBE. No, I don't.

JASON. For God's sake, you might have had the decency to tell me!

PHOEBE. You were married. You know what a stickler for form you were.

JASON. (*Uncomfortably.*) Well, you certainly kept it hidden very well.

PHOEBE. (*Calmly.*) Allison knew.

JASON. Yes—well, I don't know how she sensed that.

PHOEBE. Maybe it was the way I hung on every word you said and started to perspire when you came within two feet of me.

JASON. I have that effect on a lot of people. Anyway, I resent being the last to know.

PHOEBE. You were the first, Jason. You always knew and you enjoyed it. Oh, I can't say I blame you. You had the best of everything. Two women who adored you and had devoted their lives to satisfying your every whim. (*She turns to look at him.*) And you revelled in it.

JASON. Did you come up with that idea all by yourself?

PHOEBE. No, I went into analysis.

JASON. Why?

PHOEBE. You're an arrogant, often unfeeling, difficult man and yet for some ten years I was totally infatuated by you. I am now married to a nice, sensitive man and if my marriage was going to work, I believed it was important to come up with the reasons for my relationship with you.

JASON. (*Quietly.*) Why do you think I'm unfeeling?

PHOEBE. Jason, do you know that the only time I ever saw you cry was when a pit orchestra struck up? Never in real life.

JASON. Tears are simply the appearance of emotion. Not emotion itself.

PHOEBE. You mean you could be feeling something but it's for you to know and everyone else to find out?

JASON. What other blinding revelations did you experience?

PHOEBE. That when I found out about you and Kate Mallory I was angry with you because I really wanted you to make love with me.

JASON. You know, I liked you better before you came out of your shell.

PHOEBE. It's not easy for me to stand here and say these things, Jason.

JASON. It's not a lot of fun where I'm standing either. Look, is this encounter part of your therapy?

PHOEBE. Partly. Naturally, I wanted to find out how I would feel when I saw you.

JASON. How's it going so far?

PHOEBE. Are you just being flip or do you really want an answer?

JASON. You used to be able to tell.

PHOEBE. I also wanted to see you for professional reasons. Have you read "Romantic Comedy"?

JASON. What's that?

PHOEBE. It's the title of my book.

JASON. I'm sorry, I've been rather pressed for time lately. (*She looks at him.*) Well, don't look at me as if I haven't completed a homework assignment. I simply haven't got around to it yet.

PHOEBE. I thought you might be curious. No matter. I want to adapt it into a play and I want you to collaborate with me on it.

JASON. Why?

PHOEBE. There are two reasons. First, I'd like to tell you how I got the idea.

JASON. Is that absolutely necessary?

PHOEBE. It was a funny quote by Hemingway.

JASON. Yes, he's always cracked me up.

PHOEBE. He said that he and a woman had been in love for forty years but whenever she was single he was married and when he was single she was married. He said "we were the victims of unsynchronized passion." That started me thinking about us. I really started the book as therapy. Of course, in the writing I fantasized the relationship to make it interesting. I suppose what I'm saying is that you should write it with me because I stole your character.

JASON. Isn't this where you came in fourteen years ago?

PHOEBE. Well, that didn't turn out too badly, did it?

JASON. You said there were two reasons.

PHOEBE. The second one should be obvious. You're the best dramatist of this sort of material I know.

JASON. There's a third reason.

PHOEBE. Oh?

JASON. You think I need the money and my life is a shambles.

PHOEBE. Yes—well, I'd be less than honest if I said I

wasn't aware of that. But that has nothing—well, very little—to do with my offer. It's not your lack of money that worries me, Jason. It's your lack of spirit. You need to work.

JASON. (*Slowly rises. Icily angry.*) I am not a charity case!!

PHOEBE. I never said you were.

JASON. (*Tightly controlled.*) No, you said a lot more. Well, now let *me* say a few things. You come waltzing in here, clutching your tawdry little best seller and expect me to kiss the hem of your Givenchy dress! Well, you've made a few assumptions that need correcting. First, I may have been going through a somewhat fallow period but my career did not freeze into a "still life" the moment you left. I was writing plays when you were a teenage ticket taker and I suspect I'll be writing them long after you're a plump matron making funny speeches about your septic tank to the P.T.A. Next, your infantile psychological insights about my character and your infatuation with an unfeeling, insensitive older man. Well, I'm exactly ten years older than you, which doesn't exactly make me an aging Caesar to your pubescent Cleopatra! (*She moves to get her things.*) Wait a minute, I'm not through!

PHOEBE. I know. You haven't come up with a good exit line yet.

JASON. (*Growing ever more angry.*) Next, your concern over my alleged lack of emotion. How the hell can you presume to know what I feel or don't feel? How do you know that when you left I wasn't quite—bruised. (*She doesn't say anything. He picks up her baseball cap, waves it in front of her.*) Well, I kept your damned hat, for God's sake!! Of course, I was remembering a warm, vulnerable, compassionate, unique girl who used to blush, not the woman you've become! You know what you've become? You've become—*CRISP!* One of those confident, crisp fashion-plate bitches who think they know the secret of the world and I wouldn't work with you if you were a combination of Moliere and Mary Tyler Moore!! (*Stung, her tears are now partly from anger.*) And, since this is obviously the last time we'll ever see each other, *I was not inadequate in Chicago!!* I happened to be drunk and when a man is drunk, he—uh—he— (*He suddenly doubles over, his face contorted with pain, gasping for breath.*)

PHOEBE. What is it?

JASON. You'd better—stick around. I—think—I'm having—a heart attack. (*He collapses rather theatrically onto the floor.*)

PHOEBE. Oh, come on, Jason. We did that in "Innocent Deception" and it didn't work well there either.

JASON. (*Groaning.*) Stay with me, Phoebe.

PHOEBE. Jason? (*He doesn't answer. Uncertainly.*) Jason, don't play the fool. This is not funny. (*He turns his head towards her, breathing with difficulty. The realization hits her that he is not faking.*) Oh, my God!! (*She rushes to his side; frantically tries to find his pulse, races for a bottle of brandy, uncorks it, rushes back, kneels beside him, raises his head.*) Here—drink this brandy!

JASON. (*Feebly.*) What—what year—is it?

(PHOEBE *is giving* JASON *mouth-to-mouth resuscitation when* BLANCHE *comes in with the coffee tray.*)

BLANCHE. Well, I'm glad to see you two finally got together.

PHOEBE. Blanche, he's not breathing . . . call an ambulance.

(PHOEBE *goes back to the mouth-to-mouth,* BLANCHE *goes to the telephone as the CURTAIN FALLS.*)

END OF SCENE 1, ACT THREE

ACT THREE

SCENE 2

THE TIME: *Late afternoon three weeks later.*

AT RISE: JASON *is propped up on a pulled-out sofa bed which has replaced the sofa, with a tray across his lap, yelling for* PHOEBE. *He is wearing a robe and pajamas and is sporting a sling that supports his right wrist. The room has also been restored to its usual elegant charm.*

JASON. (*Calling.*) Phoebe! Phoebe, I need you! Phoebe!

(PHOEBE, *looking harassed and somewhat untidy, enters carrying a pile of mail.*)

PHOEBE. I heard you the first time.

JASON. I need you to cut up my food.

PHOEBE. Tapioca? (*She puts the pile of letters on the desk.*) Here's your mail.

JASON. You can read it to me later.

PHOEBE. Jason, I'm not Annie Sullivan. It's bad enough that I have to feed you. (*She takes spoon, feeds him through following.*)

JASON. Serves you right for trying to kill me.

PHOEBE. I was trying to save you.

JASON. You almost suffocated me.

PHOEBE. You should have said something.

JASON. I tried. That's when you fractured my wrist with your bony knee.

PHOEBE. Could you chew a little faster? I have about a million things to do.

JASON. You shouldn't overdo it, Phoebe. (*She looks at him.*) You're looking—I don't know—wispy.

PHOEBE. Eat.

(LEO *enters carrying a pile of telephone messages. He moves to desk with them.*)

LEO. So what do you think? Will he ever tap dance again?

JASON. I'll never eat tapioca again. What are those?

LEO. Telephone messages. I feel like a bookie.

JASON. Why has the phone stopped ringing?

LEO. I left a message on your answering service that you'd died. Thought it might slow 'em down. (*He stands, waiting.* PHOEBE *looks at him.*)

PHOEBE. Something on your mind?

LEO. Sure. Dinner.

PHOEBE. (*Annoyed.*) You're waiting for me to make it?

LEO. (*Evenly.*) No, I'll make it. I just thought it might be nice to eat together for a change.

PHOEBE. (*She is immediately contrite.*) Honey, I'm sorry. Give me about fifteen minutes.

JASON. Better make it thirty. (*They look at him.*) Phoebe has to give me my massage first. (LEO *moves towards the door.*) Oh, Leo, would you mind drawing my bath for me?

LEO. (*Turns and looks at him. We hear front DOOR-BELL.*) I have to answer the door and do the silver first. (*He exits.* PHOEBE *starts to dressing room with two bed pillows.*)

JASON. He seems a bit ticked off. Is he?

PHOEBE. Can't you tell?

JASON. Hard with Leo. He has a face like a totem pole. Probably his journalistic training. (*She looks at him but doesn't have a chance to answer as* BLANCHE *enters.*)

BLANCHE. How's "Camille" today?

PHOEBE. (*Exiting to dressing room.*) Oh, I think we can take him off the critical list.

BLANCHE. Jason, I brought the contract for you to sign. Have you read Phoebe's novel yet?

JASON. I'll try and get to it today. (*She looks at him.*) Blanche, I'm recovering from a heart attack.

BLANCHE. A *mild* heart attack.

JASON. I know. But when your heart stops beating, it's inclined to bring you up short.

BLANCHE. (*Surprised at his seriousness, she regards him for a moment.*) You okay?

JASON. (*Shrugs.*) Something like this tends to make you re-examine your life. Decide what's really important.

BLANCHE. What is important to you, Jason?

JASON. Phoebe. She always has been—I've just never admitted it to myself before. (PHOEBE *enters from dressing room carrying a portable massage table.*)

BLANCHE. You're giving him a massage?

JASON. There's a danger of my developing bed sores.

BLANCHE. You've been out of bed for days.

JASON. Well, we thought it would give me a psychological lift.

BLANCHE. Oh, we did, did we? (*To* PHOEBE.) You know what I think? I think your nurturing instinct has run amok.

JASON. Blanche, I'd appreciate it if you didn't come charging in here telling Phoebe how to run her ward. (*He exits to dressing room.* PHOEBE *closes the sofa bed through following.*)

BLANCHE. Phoebe, I hope somebody is striking a medal for you somewhere. Beyond the call and all that.

PHOEBE. There was nobody else. Besides, I felt I owed it to him.

BLANCHE. How does Leo feel about it?

PHOEBE. It was his suggestion. (*Noticing* BLANCHE'S *surprise.*) Well, we needed an apartment and Leo's a practical man. Of course I don't think he realized just how demanding a patient Jason would be. He makes Sheridan Whiteside seem like a saint. That's the character in "The Man Who Came To Dinner" who—

BLANCHE. Honey, I know who Sheridan Whiteside is. I saw the original production. (*As* PHOEBE *looks at her.*) My mother took me.

PHOEBE. I'm sorry. When I talk to Leo I have to explain any theatrical references.

BLANCHE. What do you two talk about? (PHOEBE *looks at her*.) Well, you don't seem to have a lot in common.

PHOEBE. That's my fault, not his. I've led such a narrow life, really. It wasn't until I got to Paris that I realized just how frivolous, vain and self-absorbed people in the theatre are.

BLANCHE. Missed us that much, huh? (PHOEBE *sets up the massage table*.) Listen, don't you think all this is a bit dangerous? Rekindled passion, secret yearnings—all that good stuff?

PHOEBE. Blanche, you don't really believe you only meet one person who's right just once in a lifetime?

BLANCHE. In my case—even less. Listen, honey, I married three times. Once for sex, once for money and once for good conversation. None of them are what they're cracked up to be.

PHOEBE. What else is left?

BLANCHE. Beats the hell out of me.

(JASON *enters from the dressing room with* PHOEBE's *book in his hand. He crosses directly to* BLANCHE.)

JASON. This book of Phoebe's is filthy!

BLANCHE. Are you trying to tell us you've never heard those words before?

JASON. It's not just the words. It's the sex passages. My God, they're positively pornographic!

PHOEBE. Jason, I was dealing with a young girl's fantasies about—

JASON. You really thought all those—things—about me?

PHOEBE. (*Embarrassed*.) I really would prefer we keep this discussion on a professional basis. The girl—

JASON. The girl is *you*, Phoebe!

PHOEBE. The girl is *based* upon me. The *essence* may be me—all right, it is me—but naturally I embellished—

JASON. Why are you stammering?

PHOEBE. Because I'm extremely shy. Now will you take off your clothes and lie down so I can rub you?

JASON. (*Takes off robe and reading the open book, lies stomach down on the massage table.*) Listen to this: "He had the lean hard body and supple legs of a tennis professional."

BLANCHE. So?

JASON. So that's *my* body she's describing.

PHOEBE. Don't be ridiculous, Jason. I didn't use your body.

JASON. (*Coldly.*) Oh? Why not?

PHOEBE. I wanted those passages to be erotic.

JASON. Well, it certainly *sounds* like my body— (*She is rubbing alcohol on his back.*) a few years ago. That feels good.

BLANCHE. (*Picking up her coat, purse and briefcase.*) Well, I'll leave you two alone to iron out your "creative differences." Oh, and Jason, try and be a better person. (*She exits.* PHOEBE *starts to massage* JASON'S *back as he reads.*)

JASON. (*Reading.*) "He was gracious, witty and elegant and wore the mantle of success as if it had been custom made." Well, you've certainly captured me there.

PHOEBE. I really wish you wouldn't read that out loud.

JASON. (*Reading.*) "But since he was stark naked I didn't become aware of these qualities until later. My immediate attention was caught by his—" (*She quickly pounds into his back.*) Ooof! (*She continues massaging him and* JASON *succumbs.*) Oh, that's better—oh, that feels good—yes, right there—Oh, yes. (*The door bursts open,* LEO *jumps into the room, and stands staring at them.*)

LEO. Ha-ha!!

PHOEBE. Ha-ha what?

LEO. (*Deadpan.*) I was outside the door and I heard these guttural groaning sounds and cries of pleasure. Naturally, I jumped to the conclusion that you were giving him a massage. So I burst in here—and sure enough you are. (*A beat.*) So—ha, ha!

JASON. What do you want, Leo?

LEO. I have some things to do at the desk.

JASON. Well, we're trying to work. I mean you're not going to bang a typewriter, are you?

LEO. I'll use a soft lead pencil.

(*He moves to the desk, sits, takes some papers out and starts to work. JASON and PHOEBE quickly forget he is in the room. However, LEO is very aware of the conversation and from time to time his head comes up from his work as he listens to them.*)

JASON. The ending bothers me.

PHOEBE. What?

JASON. The ending. It's too bittersweet.

PHOEBE. How would you know? You haven't read the book.

JASON. Oh, come on, Phoebe—I read the book when it was still in manuscript form.

PHOEBE. I thought so.

JASON. There are other problems.

PHOEBE. I know. Why does the girl stay in love with him all those years?

JASON. Well, I could give you a few pointers on that. He's successful, witty, charming and never boring—at least not to her.

PHOEBE. But what about the audience? He may come off as arrogant, cold and heartless. (*There is a slight pause. JASON looks at PHOEBE.*) I mean, for him to be sympathetic they have to know how he *feels* about the girl. After all, he never seems to return her feelings.

JASON. It wasn't that simple. (*A beat.*) How about this? Supposing he's a man who believes in tradition—including the tradition of marriage. As soon as he marries he realizes he's made a mistake—but he's a honorable man so he lives with his mistake—the victim of bad timing. He makes the best of the situation.

PHOEBE. You mean he wants it both ways?

JASON. Look, it wasn't easy for me—him. Selfish, yes—but isn't that human?

PHOEBE. Not enough. I mean if he really loves her, why doesn't he tell her?

JASON. All right, maybe he's a man who has trouble showing his emotions, who likes his life—especially his emotional life—as tidy as possible. Not an admirable quality—not one he admires in himself but ingrained in his character.

PHOEBE. Then why did he—

JASON. I can answer that. (*He sits, still not looking at her.*) He had the affair with the actress rather than the girl—*because* she meant nothing to him. I—he thought it would keep the situation—emotionally tidy. If it happened with the girl he knew he couldn't control it—it would have blown the roof off. (*He turns and looks at her.*) Do you believe that, Phoebe? (*There is a pause—finally* LEO *pounds the stapler startling* JASON *and* PHOEBE.) What are you doing skulking back there?

LEO. I'm sorry to have interrupted you.

PHOEBE. Oh, you haven't. (*To* JASON.) You don't want to work any more today do you?

JASON. No, I think we should call it a day. (*He moves to dressing room door, turns.*) I feel we accomplished a great deal, don't you? (*He exits.* PHOEBE *starts to fold up the massage table.*)

LEO. You need a hand with that?

PHOEBE. No, I can do it.

LEO. I'll do it . . . I'll do it. (LEO *takes table, looks at her.*)

PHOEBE. What's the matter?

LEO. It's amazing. Within three weeks he's got you back to looking like Cinderella before she went to the ball.

PHOEBE. I'm sorry, Leo. I know these last few weeks must have been very hard for you.

LEO. Just as hard for you.

PHOEBE. Well, I have been a bit distracted.

LEO. Distracted? I feel as if I've been living with a bad waitress.

PHOEBE. What do you mean?

LEO. I've been trying to catch your eye for days.

PHOEBE. (*Looks at him.*) You've caught it, honey. What's your pleasure?

LEO. When are we going to make love?

PHOEBE. (*Finally.*) Leo, I'm sorry, I—I just feel funny being in Jason and Allison's bed.

LEO. (*Evenly.*) I'm relieved to hear there's a good reason.

PHOEBE. I know it's silly but—there are a lot of memories in this house for me. Look, I've been exhausted lately. (*He doesn't say anything.*) Leo, it was your suggestion that we move in here. You had to know I'd be run ragged for a few days.

LEO. Yes, I expected all that.

PHOEBE. Then why are you so upset?

LEO. You never have to ask each other questions.

PHOEBE. (*Thrown.*) What?

LEO. You read each other's minds. It's incredible. You finish each other's sentences like—like an old married couple.

PHOEBE. It's just an old habit, Leo. We've worked together so long that we're tuned into the same wave length.

LEO. It bothers me.

PHOEBE. Why?

LEO. Because you have to ask me why! For the past fifteen minutes I've been watching my wife and a man mentally copulate. I feel like a voyeur!

PHOEBE. Leo, you're exaggerating!

JASON. (*Now fully dressed, enters.*) Listen, I've been thinking— (*He stops as he sees* LEO *and* PHOEBE *staring at one another. There is a tense pause.*) I have the feeling I've walked into the middle of a family squabble.

PHOEBE. Not at all. We—

LEO. As a matter of fact, you have.

JASON. (*Makes no effort to move.*) Well, don't let me interrupt you. (*Moving Upstage.*) I'll just sit quietly over here and read Phoebe's filthy book.

PHOEBE. We can talk about this later, Leo.

LEO. No, I think we're finished. I've decided to fly up to Rochester to see my kids.

PHOEBE. How long will you be gone?

LEO. I'll be in Rochester a few days—but I don't know how long I'll be gone.

JASON. Time for me to make a graceful exit. (*He starts for the door.*)

LEO. No, Jason. It's mine. I think you both should hear why I'm leaving. When I was about eight—don't panic, Jason, I'll cut it down to the highlights—I was a pretty fair stickball player. When the kids on my block chose up sides, I was always the second guy chosen. In high school I got straight A's. A girl named Stephanie Novak edged me out as Valedictorian. In college I was the second best distance runner in the state. The second. Are you following me?

JASON. (*Quietly.*) A pattern *is* starting to emerge.

LEO. Well, I've decided that this time I'm not going to settle for second. The others I could live with but this time I'd hate myself. And that wouldn't be fair. I'm a pretty nice guy and I don't deserve it.

PHOEBE. Leo—

LEO. (*Quietly.*) I'm almost finished. You see, it's not too bad getting the consolation prize but *being* the consolation prize really gets to me. I love you, Phoebe. I probably always will. But—I want my marriage to be a blue ribbon affair. Now I'm not exactly sure what is going on with you two—I'm not even sure you know either—but whatever it is, I think you should have a chance to find out and get it settled once and for all. To do that, you both need some time—and freedom. (*A beat.*) That's about it. (*He looks at them for a moment and then moves to door.*) I wish you happiness—one way or the other. I'd like to say you deserve each other—but I'm not sure you do. (*He exits. There is a long, tense Pause.*)

JASON. Well, he's right about one thing. He is a pretty nice guy.

PHOEBE. The hell he is.

JASON. (*Looks at her in great surprise.*) What?

PHOEBE. Who does he think he is handing me around from man to man like I'm an old football. Don't I have any say in my future?

JASON. Is that why you're angry?

PHOEBE. I'm angry because I can feel a tingling in my nose! Does that answer your question? (JASON *is too bewildered to answer.*) This means I'm either going to sneeze or cry and I have the feeling it's going to be the latter. I don't want to cry, Jason. It's embarrassing to stand here and dissolve in a flood of tears in front of you. Because I'll be honest with you, Jason. I don't like you much either. I should be expressing pure anger but my ducts are filling up—and my vision is blurring and—

JASON. Phoebe, you're not a doctor experimenting with a new drug. You don't have to keep notes.

PHOEBE. Just leave me alone. (*He hands her his silk handkerchief.*)

JASON. (*Awkwardly.*) Here. If you must cry, at least do it in style.

PHOEBE. (*Takes handkerchief.*) I'll—I'll be all right in a few minutes. My marriage has just gone down the drain and I need a few seconds to compose myself before I start a new life. I know how you hate scenes but this won't take long. You'd better avert your eyes. I'm going to give in now and cry.

JASON. (*Nervously.*) Yes—I'll—I'll clear out of your way and wait over here. (*He moves Upstage as* PHOEBE *cries. Finally.*) Feel better?

PHOEBE. Drier.

JASON. It's a start. Phoebe. (*She stops. He looks at her for a moment.*) I missed the moment again, didn't I?

PHOEBE. What?

JASON. You were right about my lacking spontaneity—one part of me standing back—always thinking of the effective gesture. And I did it again. When you were crying I should have taken you in my arms and comforted you. I wanted to—but I was too busy considering whether the staging was right—and the moment passed. (*Incredulously.*) Do you know what I said? "I'll clear out of your way and wait over here." I actually said that. Do you know that I almost didn't give you my handkerchief because it seemed cliche? What sort of man would do that? (*She doesn't answer. He comes out from behind the desk.*) Well, I don't know if the moment is right or not but— (*He marches over to her, takes her in his arms and kisses her. They break, embarrassed.*)

PHOEBE. Well, I suppose some decisions have to be reached.

JASON. I suppose they do.

PHOEBE. What would you like for dinner?

JASON. Could we begin with something easier?

PHOEBE. I'll get it started. (*She moves towards the door.*) —I just think you should know—I don't have the faintest idea of how to go about this thing. (*They are gazing at one another as the CURTAIN FALLS.*)

END OF SCENE 2, ACT THREE

ACT THREE

Scene 3

Time: *The next morning.*

At Rise: Jason *and* Phoebe *are sharing the sofa bed.* Jason *is asleep,* Phoebe, *in his robe, is looking lovingly at him.* Jason *wakes and turns to her.*

PHOEBE. (*Finally.*) So—how do you like your eggs?
JASON. (*Turns to look at her.*) You *know* how I like them.
PHOEBE. Scrambled? (*He nods. A small pause.*) How did you sleep?
JASON. Fine. (*A beat.*) How about you?
PHOEBE. Very well, thank you.
JASON. Good.
PHOEBE. Well—I'll get breakfast started. (*She kisses him lightly, gets out of bed, picks up her clothes and moves to door.*)
JASON. You need any help?
PHOEBE. No, I can manage, thanks.
JASON. I'll tidy up the room.
PHOEBE. Good. (*She smiles a trifle too brightly.*) Well—

(*She rather awkwardly blows him a kiss and exits.* JASON *gets out of bed, calmly puts on his trousers and shirt. He is in the middle of buttoning up his shirt when he lets out a low, anguished moan.*)

JASON. That—was—the—most—*embarrassing experience of my life!!!* (*He goes into the same maniacal dance we saw him execute in the first scene, jerkily moving around the room suffused with a combination of frustration and embarrassment.*) God, that was—awful! Absolutely, utterly— horrendous! Humiliating! *The* most humil— (*He stops as he sees* PHOEBE *who has re-entered and is staring at him. There is a pause.*) I really wish you wouldn't keep doing that.

PHOEBE. (*Finally.*) There's a hippopotamus in the room, isn't there?

JASON. (*Uncomfortably.*) Maybe if we ignore it, it'll go away.

PHOEBE. I don't think so. (*He looks at her.*) Jason, I think we should discuss it openly and frankly.

JASON. What?

PHOEBE. Our—"you know" life.

JASON. Well, that's certainly being frank.

PHOEBE. (*She clears her throat. Firmly.*) All right. Jason, I don't want you to feel bad because I didn't have an orgasm.

JASON. (*Looks at her for a moment.*) Well, I don't want you to feel bad because I didn't have one either. (*She doesn't smile.*) And as your cousin would say—ha-ha.

PHOEBE. Was it because of something I did—or didn't do?

JASON. (*Uncomfortably.*) Of course not. Why would you think that?

PHOEBE. Sometimes I get—overexcited. (*Somewhat baffled, he looks at her. She nervously clears her throat.*) I mean I tend to have trouble accepting—the gift of sensuality and I get so anxious to please I come off as—an overeager puppy dog. You know, all wet tongue and wagging tail.

JASON. Sounds pretty good to me. Oh, Phoebe, it's not you— (*Awkwardly.*) Look, I think we're overreacting to the whole—situation. It—it was fine.

PHOEBE. Fine?

JASON. Fine.

PHOEBE. (*Quietly.*) Jason, after fourteen years and two wrecked marriages, "fine" doesn't quite make it.

JASON. (*Awkwardly—gently.*) There was a lot of pressure on us to—succeed.

PHOEBE. (*Looks at him for a moment. Briskly.*) All right, let's try and put that in perspective first. On a scale of ten would you say we're a five?

JASON. I can see why you were so popular as a teacher. You're an easy grader.

PHOEBE. Oh, my God.

JASON. What?

PHOEBE. I thought it was just me. I expected you to reassure me, tell me that it wasn't important.

JASON. I did.

PHOEBE. I didn't believe you.

JASON. I'm sorry, kid.

PHOEBE. (*Finally.*) It's funny, isn't it?

JASON. What?

PHOEBE. Us. Twelve years of pent-up passion and it didn't end with a bang—but with a whimper.

JASON. And very few of them. (*Gently.*) We're about fourteen years out of sync, kid.

PHOEBE. Our timing's *that* bad?

JASON. We should have become lovers when we met— but that wasn't possible. So, over the years, I lived through your cold sores and you suffered through my post nasal drip. I held your head when you threw up on opening nights and you gave me sponge baths when I was sick. In short, my friend—we became friends.

PHOEBE. You don't think it's possible to have a good sex life with a friend?

JASON. I don't know. You're the first friend I've been to bed with.

PHOEBE. (*Finally.*) You know, after everything that's happened, after everything we've been through—people expect us to get married.

JASON. To hell with them. Let 'em find their own happy ending. That's the first time I've seen you actually *cry* at one of my jokes.

PHOEBE. (*Tearfully.*) It's just that we seem to have made

such a mess of everything. (*We hear the front DOORBELL RING.*)

JASON. We're not the only people in the world with bad timing. (*He gets up,* PHOEBE *moves to the door, turns.*)

PHOEBE. What are we going to do, Jason?

(*They are looking at one another uncertainly as the DOOR-BELL RINGS again. She exits.* JASON *folds the sofa bed. After a moment* LEO *enters. The two men look at one another.*)

LEO. (*Finally.*) So how's it going?

JASON. Fine.

LEO. Phoebe's getting the rest of my stuff.

JASON. Where are you off to this time?

LEO. Spain. I though I'd take some time off to write a book.

JASON. Why not? Everyone else is. Inside story stuff?

LEO. Fiction. Phoebe taught me a lot.

JASON. Do you regret having married her, Leo?

LEO. Of course not.

JASON. Do you mind if I ask you a personal question?

LEO. (*Dryly.*) I look on you as practically a member of the family.

JASON. How was your sex life?

LEO. (*Finally.*) You mean did the earth move?

JASON. Actually, I'd like you to be more specific than that.

LEO. Shouldn't we go into the locker room for this discussion?

JASON. Look, I'm not enjoying the tenor of this conversation, either. I wouldn't ask if it weren't important. (LEO *takes out his notebook and starts to write.*) What are you writing?

LEO. Specifics. I thought if I put it in a questionnaire form it would be easier for you to refer to.

JASON. Sometimes I find your dry humor irritating.

LEO. (*Still typing.*) Did it ever occur to you that I might be embarrassed, too? Don't let these clothes fool you. I'm not as sophisticated as I look. (LEO *tears the page out of the notebook and hands it to* JASON.)

JASON. You're sure you're not exaggerating?

LEO. (*A beat.*) I'm only working from memory, of course.

JASON. (*Caustically.*) It's obviously extremely vivid.

LEO. Yes.

(*The two men are staring at one another as* PHOEBE, *now dressed, enters. There is an awkward moment.*)

PHOEBE. (*Awkwardly.*) So—what have you two been talking about?

LEO. Phoebe, you want to come to Spain with me?

PHOEBE. (*Finally—shakily.*) You think I just bounce from bed to bed like Nell Gwyn?

LEO. I think it's about time you grew up.

PHOEBE. How do I do that?

LEO. Come with me. Nothing's been lost, Phoebe.

PHOEBE. Oh?

LEO. (*Shrugs.*) Everybody has someone in their past they wonder about. All very romantic. But the very notion of romantic love demands that it be unrequited. So requited isn't what it's supposed to be. Things didn't turn out the way you'd planned. It happens to all of us.

JASON. (*Agitated.*) Look, if you've finished playing "the old philosopher." Aren't you assuming a lot? How can you possibly know it didn't turn out as planned?

LEO. (*Losing his temper.*) Because there's no way it could! Nothing could have lived up to the sort of expectations you both had!

JASON. (*Rising.*) Did it ever occur to you that we might just be in love with each other?

LEO. Oh, come off it! You're not in love with each other! You're in love with the magic of make believe!

JASON. Then why the hell did you leave us alone together? (*There is a slight pause as* LEO *regains control.*)

LEO. There was a good reason for that. Stupidity. It wasn't until last night that I realized how *stupid* I'd been. You had me playing a role—the noble husband who steps aside so that his wife can find "true romantic fulfillment." I mean what a bullshit thing to do!

JASON. (*Mildly.*) I thought it was rather a nice touch myself.

LEO. Is that supposed to be funny?

JASON. Well, I'm sorry if I'm not up to my usual form. You see I have this feeling I'm about to see a fourteen year old dream of mine destroyed. I've had it a long time! I've grown attached to it!

LEO. Yes, well I'm a reporter. I deal in the here and now. (*To* PHOEBE.) I'm not in love with the way you were fourteen years ago—or five years ago. I love the woman you are now—today. I want you exactly as you are. (*A pause.*) Is it so hard to choose between us, Phoebe?

PHOEBE. (*Shakily.*) You're looking at a girl who couldn't even get a date on Saturday night. A very conventional girl.

LEO. Forget about conventions. Look, both Jason and I want what is best for you, but we can't decide that *for* you. Whatever you decide—we'll accept. For once in your life be selfish. (*She looks over at* JASON.)

JASON. (*Finally—somewhat harshly.*) He's right.

PHOEBE. (*Hurt.*) Don't you love me?

JASON. (*Looks at her for a moment. Gently.*) Phoebe, do you remember "Innocent Deception"? On paper everything seemed perfect but for some reason it just didn't work. The chemistry wasn't there. It *should* have worked, we *wanted* it to work but—it just didn't.

PHOEBE. (*Tightly.*) So much for happy endings.

JASON. Welcome to real life, kid. Take care of her, Leo. (*He moves away.*)

LEO. I'll get your things and grab a cab. (LEO *exits*.)

PHOEBE. If I walk out of that door it won't solve all our problems, you know. All our lives—somehow we'll always be—connected.

JASON. (*Turns to look at her.*) Phoebe, you have a nasty little romantic streak in you that pops out at the slightest provocation.

PHOEBE. Look who's talking. (*A beat.*) And there's not an orchestra pit within miles.

JASON. Before you go there is something that should be said. (*A beat.*) I love you, Phoebe. I always have. And when you came back and it seemed you didn't feel the same way about me—I still loved you. I suppose that was the clincher. I'm a very selfish man and the fact that I could love someone without getting anything in return— (*A slight shrug.*) Then when I woke up this morning—after everything had not been what we'd both wanted—you were still my best friend. I find that—extraordinary.

PHOEBE. (*Finally.*) So do I. (PHOEBE *exits.* JASON *stands for a moment regarding the room. He moves up to the desk and looks again around the room. In the distance we hear the FRONT DOOR SLAM.* JASON *slumps over his desk chair. There is a pause and then* PHOEBE *reenters.*) You're miscast as Sydney Carton you know.

JASON. Oh, I don't know. You're back aren't you?

PHOEBE. Aren't you going to ask what happened?

JASON. (*Turns to face her.*) I know what happened. Friendship 1, Lust 0. Right?

PHOEBE. Well, I wouldn't put it *quite* that way.

JASON. How would you put it?

PHOEBE. I never quite got the hang of real life.

JASON. That's why you came back?

PHOEBE. No. Where else would I find someone as hopelessly outdated as I am? (*They smile at one another for a moment.*) You working on the last scene?

JASON. Just doodling.

PHOEBE. (*Moves into the room. Briskly.*) All right. This couple have gone through the equivalent of a marriage. They finally get together only to discover the only thing they have left is—what?

JASON. A mutual lack of passion.

PHOEBE. (*Quickly.*) I'm very passionate about you!

JASON. (*Gently.*) And I about you. (*They look at one another for a moment.*) We seem to be off the subject. They're left with—what?

PHOEBE. A mutuality of interests. They go to movies, museums, ball games together. They grow old together— good companions. It's sweet.

JASON. It's depressing.

PHOEBE. It could be romantic—in a funny way.

JASON. Funny is good. (JASON *crosses and sits on the sofa.*) I've been thinking. Given the basic talent—and I'm sure they both have that—sex can be learned. I mean you weren't a very good writer when you came to me but, with a little instruction, look how well you turned out.

PHOEBE. If I run I could still catch Leo.

JASON. It would give them a common interest. Like learning a common language.

PHOEBE. Are you through?

JASON. I think so.

PHOEBE. (*Sits on sofa, taking* JASON's *feet on her lap.*) None of that is important. The important thing is friendship. I mean anyone can find a good sex partner. You found it with Allison. I found it with Leo. (*She is now stroking his leg under his trouser cuffs, too absorbed with what she is saying to realize the effect it is having on* JASON.) But a true, loving friendship between a man and a woman where you accept one another's faults and still like the other— that's rare and valuable. *That's* what's important.

JASON. I agree.

PHOEBE. (*Thoughtfully.*) Of course it would be nice to have sex too.

JASON. Come over here, Phoebe.

PHOEBE. Shouldn't we keep working?

JASON. We'll improvise.

PHOEBE. (*Moves to lie down beside him, her head on his chest.*) I thought you hated improvisation.

JASON. I'm willing to learn. (*She is now moving into his arms.*) It's not going to work with your elbow in my rib cage.

PHOEBE. Well, if you'd hold your head—

JASON. No—see if you do that I can't breathe.

PHOEBE. No wonder this sort of thing always happens offstage.

JASON. It doesn't have to be a *ballet,* Phoebe. Just . . .

PHOEBE. Wait a minute—I have a better idea. (*She moves on top of* JASON.)

JASON. You really want to do it that way?

PHOEBE. Well, I think we should at least try it.

JASON. Yes, but it cuts off all circulation to my—knees! (*The curtain starts to fall.*)

PHOEBE. Jason, stop talking and—collaborate. (*The CURTAIN IS IN.*)

THE END

PROPERTY PLOT

ACT ONE, SCENE 1

D.R. bar

  on bar: 2 lamps

    brandy bottle

    3 brandy glasses

    4 liqueur glasses

    sherry decanter

    whiskey decanter

    tray: ice bucket

      scotch decanter

      vodka decanter

      6 old-fashioned glasses

    decanter

    bottle of vermouth

R. of C. sofa with Chinese cover and seven pillows, board, 2
  striped sheets

right arm of sofa: navy blue suit

left arm of sofa: navy blue suit

behind sofa: sofa table with flowers

left of sofa: bench

front of sofa: coffee table with 2 mags., art book, cig. box,
  3 scripts (one blue which is "girl in the back seat")

on shelf U.R.: 1 pin stripe suit hanging

cabinet under bookshelf: typewriter case, telephone books

U.C. on platform: desk

  on desk:

    white typing paper on blotter and left and right of blotter

    brass desk calender

    gray letter holder

    brown letter holder

    pencil sharpener (D.L. corner)

    lamp

    telephone D.R. corner

> unopened mail (by telephone)
> stapler
> letter opener
> pencil holder with yellow pencils, felt pens
> Chinese vase

behind desk: desk chair pushed up to desk
U.S.R. of desk: wastebasket
U.S.R. in cabinet:
> top shelf:
>> typing paper
>> 3 boxes
>> letters with rubber band around them
> bottom shelf:
>> box of file folders

U.S.C. cabinet: on top 8 scripts
D.L.C. wing chair
> on chair: pin strip suit

front of chair: footstool
S.L. of chair: Pembroke table
> on table:
>> lamp
>> blue vase
>> 3 small pictures
>> silver ashtray

U.L.C. library steps
U.L. round table with pictures, lamp, flowers
preset off right:
> suit on hanger (wardrobe)
> 5 ties (1 wardrobe)
> shirt (wardrobe)
> shorts (wardrobe)
> shoes (wardrobe)
> rolled socks (wardrobe)
> cuff link box with cuff links (1 pair wardrobe)
> folder newspaper
> 2 glasses with small amount of liquor

massage table
blue towel
white towel
white sheet
baby oil
glass with 2 pill bottles in it
small tray coffee table
suitcase
book
book ''Romantic Comedy''
fish bowl with fish
cup and saucer that matches tea set
basket with 3 balls of yarn, knitting needles with knitting
basket with children's clothes
wastebasket
stack of books
2 file boxes
   in boxes:
      pencil holder with yellow pencils and felt pens
      tensor lamp
      gold fish food
      file rack
      file folders
      clip board with yellow pad
      tape recorder
      picture of children
      pair of jeans with patch and needle
      3 paper back books
      1 script in folder
      5 scripts
      newspaper
      paper clip holder
      box of push pins
      box of kleenex & sewing basket
bulletin board with dressing
3 children's shirts

#1 box
    pajamas
    2 shirts
    stack of newspapers
    4 magazines
  2 pillows with striped cases
  Louis XV chair
preset trees: green ones on marks
preset off left:
  report card
  folder (LEO)
  8 telephone messages
  3 cloth samples
  car robe
  small coffee table
  briefcase with pen clipped to seperater, date book with
    contracts in center, brown folder, file folder with papers
  pillow with white case
  tan carrobe
  white sheet
  silver tray with coffee pot with coffee, 3 cups and
    saucers, sugar bowl, cream pitcher, spoon
  tray with tea pot with tea, spoon, plate with cookies,
    sugar bowl, cream pitcher
  paper bag with Chinese soup container with soup, nap-
    kin, spoon
  breakfast tray with bowl, spoon, cup and saucer all match
  tea set; in rack on tray: 2 magazines, sling
  2 blue scripts
  newspaper
  vase with red flowers
  box #1:
    4 pair of half glasses
    brief case
    2 yellow pads
    2 scripts in folders

    tea cup with saucer
    5 sheets of yellow paper with writing and paper clip
    5 sheets of yellow paper without clip
    large book
    pencil
box #2:
    tray
    glass coffee pot
    2 pottery cups
    1 pottery plate
    1 glass
    yogurt container
    1 small Chinese container
    1 large Chinese container
    chip bag
    cookie bag
    coke can
    sweater
    stack of newspapers
    5 magazines
    empty pizza carton
    juice bottle
    3 coffee containers
    3 pieces of crumpled yellow paper
    2 scripts in envelopes
    peanut can
preset in change room: KATE's coat and purse
check PHOEBE's dresser: letter, small clip board, 2 pair of
    eye glasses, blue script, running suit, baseball hat, 8
    unopened get well cards, Barnes and Nobel shopping bag
    with paper back books, shopping bag with stuffing
personal: notebook and pencil (LEO)
dressing room door open
ACT ONE, SCENE 2
set from stage right:
    glass with liquor on coffee table

newspaper on sofa

strike from stage right:

    glass from coffee table

    glass from bar

    flowers from sofa table

    hangers from sofa table

    massage table from right of sofa

    cuff link box from sofa table

    glass from sofa table

set from stage left:

    car robe on footstool

    red flowers on round table

strike from stage left:

    flowers from round table

    purse, coat, 2 shopping bags from chair left

during SCENE 2: get 3 glasses from stage right and 1 glass
      from stage left wash and put in cartons in box #1 stage
      left

ACT TWO, SCENE 1

strike:

    red flowers to stage left

    chair and footstool to stage left

    blanket, pillow, sheet to stage left

    top of round table to stage left

    art book, 2 magazines, 3 scripts, cig. box off coffee table
      to stage right

    coffee table to stage right

    bench to stage left

    2 brandy glasses to stage left

    silver tray with coffee service to stage left

    1 low ball glass to stage left

    pillows and sofa cover from sofa to stage right

    green trees

set:

    bare trees

    D.R. small tray table with file holder with files in it above
      small table Pembroke table

on table:

tensor lamp
2 paper back books
gold fish bowl
gold fish food
kleenex
paper clip holder
box of push pins
bulletin board
script in manila folder
file box

above Pembroke 2 file cartons with 5 scripts and stack books

right of Pembroke: chair on chair: blue jeans with needle

front of chair: footstool on footstool and open sewing basket open

right of footstool 2 baskets one with knitting and the other with children clothes, tape recorder

left of chair small tray table

on table:

clip board with yellow pad
pencil holder with pencils and pens
cup and saucer

U.R. library steps

D.R.C. Louis XV chair with JASON's jacket

R. of chair round table

on table: half eye glasses, large history book, dictaphone, 3 small pictures, tapes

U.C. desk

add to desk: briefcase, half eye glasses, yellow pad, script in manila folder, 5 sheets of yellow paper with paper clip, black lamp

check on desk: stapler, unopened mail

above desk: desk chair pushed against desk

right of desk: typing table with typewriter

D.L. sofa with brown seat and *pillows*

above sofa: sofa table with pictures from round table,
    1 pair of half glasses, lamp

front of sofa: coffee table with silver tray with teapot,
    plate with cookies, cup, cream pitcher, sugar bowl,
    1 pair of half eye glasses, 5 sheets of yellow paper
    with paper clip, 5 sheets of yellow paper loose, pencil

U.L. bar: same as Act One with 4 clean glasses, orange
    flower arrangement

ACT TWO, SCENE 2

set from stage right:

    KATE's coat and purse (wardrobe)

    3 children's shirts to left side of footstool

strike from stage right:

    script in manila folder from Pembroke table

    sewing basket from footstool to floor

    cup and saucer from small table left of chair

strike from stage left:

    tray from coffee table, flowers from bar

    script in manila folder from coffee table

    script in manila folder and teacup from desk

set from stage left:

    blue script on coffee table

    blue script on desk

during scene 2:

    set warm-up suit and baseball hat on prop table stage right

    make soup, fix yogurt and applesauce in small dish on
        breakfast tray

    set teapot, cream pitcher, sugar bowl on breakfast tray

during scene 1:

    wash coffee pot and 2 cups and brandy glasses

ACT THREE, SCENE 1

strike:

    suitcase to stage right (get stapler from suitcase put on
        desk)

    sofa pillows stage left

    board from sofa stage left

things left D.R. stage right

bulletin board D.R. stage right

typewriter case to cabinet U.R.

paper, pencil boxes, small white boxes to U.L. cabinet
behind desk

cloth sample from desk

set:

yellow trees

D.R. wall: Louis XV chair on floor in front of chair:
pajamas

U.S. chair: Pembroke table with pictures from sofa table,
lamp, 5 magazines

U.S.R. library steps
on steps: raincoat (wardrobe), 2 shirts

U.R. bookcase: baseball cap

R.C. chair with footstool: right of chair stack of newspapers

stage right of chair: stack of newspapers

L. of chair: round table
on table: glass coffee pot, plate, mug

D.S.C. telephone on floor with receiver of floor

check stapler on desk

wastebasket moved D.S.R. on platform with 3 pieces of
crumpled yellow paper

couch moved to Act Three marks car robe on stage left
arm, 5 magazines on sofa

sofa table: lamp, 1 pair of half glasses

S.L. of sofa table: sweater on floor

front of sofa: coffee table
on coffee table:
tray with can of coke, peanut can, juice bottle, plate,
coffee mug, dirty glass, cookie bag, Frito bag,
3 coffee containers, 2 Chinese food containers,
yogurt container

on floor right of coffee table: pizza carton

D.R. of door on floor: stack of newspapers

special note: D.S. of dressing room door stack of newspapers under Pembroke table 2 shopping bags on
platform shopping bag

ACT THREE, SCENE 2

set from stage right:

2 pillows with stripped cases

small tray table with glass and two pill bottles

strike from stage right:

pajamas from D.R. chair

shirts from library table

shopping bags from under Pembroke table

stack of newspapers from D.R. of door

glass, soup container from round table

brandy bottle from floor center

set from stage left:

small tray table with newspaper

breakfast tray

open bed

telephone to small table right of sofa

strike from stage left:

dump wastebasket and put outside of door

papers from D.R. of door

tray from sofa table

lap robe from sofa

sweater from sofa table

briefcase from sofa

shopping bag from platform

cape, 2 pair of gloves, 2 purses, from sofa

coffee table

ACT THREE, SCENE 3

set from stage left: 2 stripped pillows

set from stage left: open bed, PHOEBE's clothes

strike from stage left: small tray table

Special Note: PHOEBE's glasses (2 pair), small clip board
with yellow pad, blue script, letter from BLANCHE,
8 unopened letters to wardrobe as used

COSTUME LIST

JASON
ACT ONE, SCENE 1
   blue robe with red piping
   cream silk shirt
   taupe slacks
   brown leather slippers
   blue silk ascot
   navy 2 piece suit
   black lace-up shoes
   white French cuff shirt
   Yale club tie
   black socks
   white boxer shorts
ACT ONE, SCENE 2
   black tuxedo
   repeat white shirt, shoes, socks
   black bow tie
   black chesterfield coat
   white silk scarf
   silk handkerchief
   gold brocade dressing gown
ACT TWO, SCENE 1
   buscuit suede jacket
   brown tweed slacks
   brown loafers
   brown tweed socks
   blue tattersall shirt
   handkerchief
   3 piece grey plaid suit
   pink shirt
   black knit tie
   black shoes
   black socks

ACT TWO, Scene 2
    brown 3 piece tweed suit
    putty shirt
    brown loafers
    brown socks
    tie
ACT THREE, Scene 1
    navy aged cardigan
    brown aged slacks
    checked shirt
    brown suede slippers
    brown socks
ACT THREE, Scene 2
    navy robe
    stripped pajamas
    sling
    brown suede slippers
    handkerchief
ACT THREE, Scene 3
    brown slacks
    dark plaid shirt
    brown loafers
    brown socks
    silk handkerchief
PHOEBE
ACT ONE, Scene 1
    green/blue skirt
    liberty print blouse
    navy blue cardigan
    green knee socks
    brown loafers
    trenchcoat
    tote bag
ACT ONE, Scene 2
    tea-colored party dress
    matching evening shoes
    evening bag

pearl necklace
raincoat and hat

ACT TWO, Scene 1
navy sweat pants
yellow sweat shirt
running shoes
socks
baseball cap

ACT TWO, Scene 2
green loden coat
red/green plaid pleated skirt
sweater vest
stripped blouse
brown boots
knit hat
knit scarf
shoulder bag
knit gloves

ACT THREE, Scene 1
purple morie blouse
black velvet skirt
black fox boa
black hat and gloves
black hat
pearl earrings

ACT THREE, Scene 2
blue jeans
blue stripped blouse
grey cardigan
brown short boots

ACT THREE, Scene 3
JASON's blue robe
rose silk blouse
deep plum skirt
plum leather belt
taupe shoes

BLANCHE

ACT ONE, SCENE 1
   pink chiffon dress
   pink satin bow hat
   pink shoes
   purse and gloves
   pearl earrings

ACT ONE, SCENE 2
   green evening dress
   dark mink coat
   green purse and gloves
   black evening pumps
   earrings

ACT TWO, SCENE 2
   brown wool coat dress
   brown suede boots
   brown suede bag
   brown mink cape

ACT THREE, SCENE 1
   red/black jersey dress with matching cape
   red/black bag and gloves
   black suede shoes

ACT THREE, SCENE 2
   brown satin dress with fur trim
   brown suede shoes
   repeat brown suede bag and gloves

ALLISON

ACT ONE, SCENE 1
   ivory wedding gown and veil
   white shoes
   white gloves
   pearl earrings

ACT ONE, SCENE 2
   blue brocade dress
   blue satin toque hat
   blue shoes and bag
   sable coat

blue dressing gown
blue slippers
ACT TWO, SCENE 1
   orange 2 piece knit suit
   melon blouse
   taupe suede shoes
ACT TWO, SCENE 2
   beige checked dress
   taupe blouse
   taupe suede shoes
KATE MALLORY
ACT TWO, SCENE 2
   green inside-out dress
   taupe shoes
   pearl necklace
   mink coat
   brown bag
LEO
ACT TWO, SCENE 1
   grey slacks
   grey Harris tweed jacket
   cream shirt with rust stripe
   brown knit tie
   brown suede Hush Puppies
   brown socks
   tan loden coat
ACT THREE, SCENE 2
   grey corduroy suit
   blue tattersall shirt
   blue knit sweater vest
   tan Wallabees
   grey socks
ACT THREE, SCENE 3
   repeat slacks from suit, shoes, socks
   green turtleneck sweater
   tan loden coat

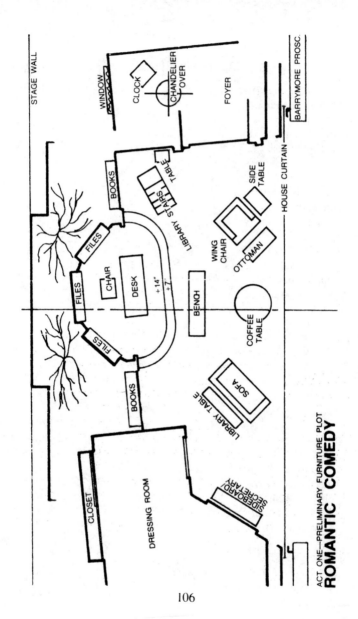

ACT ONE—PRELIMINARY FURNITURE PLOT
ROMANTIC COMEDY

106

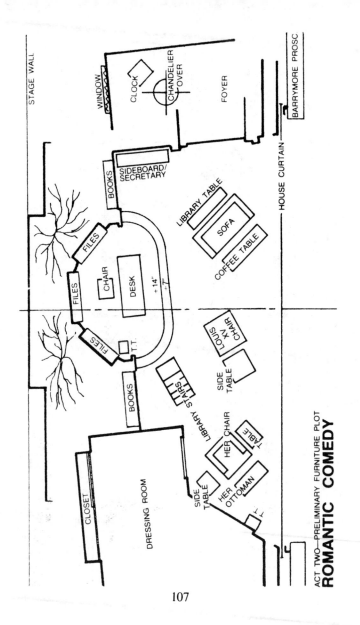

ACT TWO—PRELIMINARY FURNITURE PLOT
ROMANTIC COMEDY

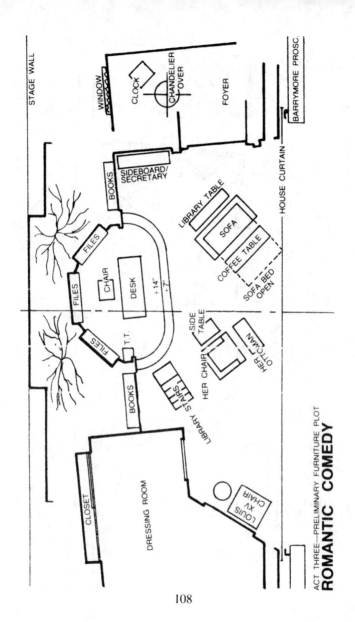

ACT THREE—PRELIMINARY FURNITURE PLOT
ROMANTIC COMEDY

108

NEW MUSICALS

from

SAMUEL FRENCH, INC.

BALLROOM – THE BEST LITTLE WHOREHOUSE
IN TEXAS – CHICAGO – CHRISTMAS IS COMIN'
UPTOWN – THE CLUB – COLE – THE DRACULA
SPECTACULAR – DRACULA: THE *MUSICAL?* –
FESTIVAL – THE FIRST – GOLD DUST –
HAPPY END – HAPPY NEW YEAR – HIJINKS! –
A HISTORY OF THE AMERICAN FILM – I LOVE MY
WIFE – I'M GETTING MY ACT TOGETHER AND
TAKING IT ON THE ROAD – JERRY'S GIRLS –
KURT VONNEGUT'S GOD BLESS YOU MR.
ROSEWATER – MARCH OF THE FALSETTOS –
MUSICAL CHAIRS – MY OLD FRIENDS –
THE 1940'S RADIO HOUR – OH, BROTHER!
ON THE TWENTIETH CENTURY – OPERETTA –
PETTICOAT LANE – PIAF – PIANO BAR –
THE PICTURE OF DORIAN GRAY – PUMP BOYS
AND DINETTES – THE ROCKY HORROR SHOW –
RUNAWAYS – THE SALOONKEEPER'S DAUGHTER –
THE SEVEN – STRIDER – SUGAR BABIES –
THEY'RE PLAYING OUR SONG – TRIXIE TRUE,
TEEN DETECTIVE – UNSUNG COLE (AND
CLASSICS, TOO) – THE UTTER GLORY OF
MORRISSEY HALL – THE WIZ – WOMAN
OVERBOARD – YOU NEVER KNOW

*For descriptions of these and all our musicals consult our Musicals
Catalogue*

FAVORITE

BROADWAY COMEDIES
from
SAMUEL FRENCH, INC.

BAREFOOT IN THE PARK – BEDROOM FARCE –
BLITHE SPIRIT – BUTTERFLIES ARE FREE –
CALIFORNIA SUITE – CHAMPAGNE COMPLEX –
CHAPTER TWO – COME BLOW YOUR HORN – DA –
THE GINGERBREAD LADY – GOD'S FAVORITE –
THE GOOD DOCTOR – HAPPY BIRTHDAY,
WANDA JUNE – HAY FEVER – HOW THE OTHER
HALF LOVES – I OUGHT TO BE IN PICTURES –
JUMPERS – KNOCK KNOCK – LAST OF THE RED
HOT LOVERS – MY FAT FRIEND – NEVER TOO LATE
– NIGHT AND DAY – THE NORMAN CONQUESTS –
NORMAN, IS THAT YOU? – THE ODD COUPLE –
OTHERWISE ENGAGED – THE OWL AND THE
PUSSYCAT – THE PRISONER OF 2ND AVENUE –
THE PRIVATE EAR AND THE PUBLIC EYE –
THE RAINMAKER – SAME TIME, NEXT YEAR –
THE SHOW OFF – 6 RMS RIV VU – THE SUNSHINE
BOYS – A THOUSAND CLOWNS – TRAVESTIES –
TWIGS – TWO FOR THE SEASAW

*For descriptions of these and all our plays, consult our Basic
Catalogue of Plays.*

Other Publications for Your Interest

GROWN UPS

(LITTLE THEATRE—COMEDY)

By JULES FEIFFER

2 men, 3 women, 1 female child—Interiors

An acerbic comedy by the famed cartoonist and author of *Knock Knock* and *Little Murders*. It's about a middle-aged journalist who has, at last, grown-up—only to find he's trapped in a world of emotional infants. "A laceratingly funny play about the strangest of human syndromes—the love that kills rather than comforts. Feiffer's vision seems merciless, but its mercy is the fierce comic clarity with which he exposes every conceivable permutation of smooth-tongued cruelty . . . Feiffer constructs a fiendishly complex machine of reciprocal irritation in which Jake (the journalist), his parents, his wife and his sister carp, cavil, harass, hector and finally attack one another with relentless trivia that detonate deeply buried resentments like emotional land mines . . . Moving past Broadway one-liners and easy gags, (Feiffer) makes laughter an adventure . . . This farce is Feiffer's exclusive specialty, and it's never been more harrowingly hilarious."—Newsweek. "Savagely funny."—N.Y. Times. "A compelling, devastating evening of theatre . . . the first adult play of the season."—Women's Wear Daily.   (#9125)

LUNCH HOUR

(LITTLE THEATRE—COMEDY)

By JEAN KERR

3 men, 2 women—Interior

Never has Jean Kerr's wit had a keener edge or her comic sense more peaks of merriment than in this clever confection, starring Gilda Radner and Sam Waterston as a pair whose spouses are having an affair, and who have to counter by inventing an affair of their own. He, ironically, is a marriage counsellor, and a bit of a stick. His wife juggles husband, lover and mother and is a real go-getter. In fact, it was she who proposed to him. Of the other couple, the wife is a bit kooky. She can discourse on things tacky while wearing an evening gown with her jogging sneakers on; or, again, be overjoyed at the prospect of a trip to Paris: "And we'll never have to ask for french fried potatoes. They'll just come like that." While her husband, "Well, he's rich for a living." Or as he expresses it: "It's very difficult to do something if you don't need any money." All ends forgivingly for both couples, as the aggrieved wife concedes that they both "need something to regret," and the other husband concedes "I knew when I married that everyone would want to dance with you." "Civilized, charming, stylish . . . Very warm and most amusing . . . delicately interweaves laughter and romance."—N.Y. Times. "An amiable comedy about the eternal quadrangle . . . The author's most entertaining play in years."—N.Y. Daily News. "A beautiful weave of plot, character and laughs . . . It's delicious."—NBC-TV.   (#674)

Other Publications for Your Interest

SOCIAL SECURITY
(LITTLE THEATRE—COMEDY)

By ANDREW BERGMAN

3 men, 3 women—Interior

This is a real, honest-to-goodness hit Broadway comedy, as in the Good Old Days of Broadway. Written by one of Hollywood's top comedy screenwriters ("Blazing Saddles" and "The Inlaws") and directed by the great Mike Nichols, this hilarious comedy starred Marlo Thomas and Ron Silver as a married couple who are art dealers. Their domestic tranquility is shattered upon the arrival of the wife's goody-goody nerd of a sister, her up-tight CPA husband and her Archetypal Jewish Mother. They are there to try to save their college student daughter from the horrors of living only for sex. The comic sparks really begin to fly when the mother hits it off with the elderly minimalist artist who is the art dealers' best client! "Just when you were beginning to think you were never going to laugh again on Broadway, along comes *Social Security* and you realize, with a rising feeling of joy, that it is once more safe to giggle in the streets. Indeed, you can laugh out loud, joyfully, with, as it were, social security, for the play is a hoot, and better yet, a sophisticated, even civilized hoot."—NY Post.   (#21255)

ALONE TOGETHER
(LITTLE THEATRE—COMEDY)

By LAWRENCE ROMAN

4 men, 2 women—Interior

Remember those wonderful Broadway comedies of the fifties and sixties, such as *Never Too Late* and *Take Her, She's Mine*? This new comedy by the author of *Under the Yum Yum Tree* is firmly in that tradition. Although not a hit with Broadway's jaded critics, *Alone Together* was a delight with audiences. On Broadway Janis Paige and Kevin McCarthy played a middle aged couple whose children have finally left the nest. They are now alone together—but not for long. All three sons come charging back home after experiencing some Hard Knocks in the Real World—and Mom and Dad have quite a time pushing them out of the house so they can once again be *alone together.* "Mr. Roman is a fast man with a funny line."—Chr. Sci. Mon. "A charmer."—Calgary Sunday Sun. "An amiable comedy . . . the audience roared with recognition, pleasure and amusement."—Gannett Westchester Newsp. "Delightfully wise and witty." Hollywood Reporter. "One of the funniest shows we've seen in ages."—Herald-News. TV.   (#238)